you, lord?

when did
we see

chiara lubich

when did we see you, lord?

new city press, new york

Published in the United States by New City Press
the Publishing House of the Focolare Movement, Inc.
206 Skillman Avenue, Brooklyn, N.Y. 11211
© 1979 by New City Press, Brooklyn, N.Y.
Translated from the original Italian edition
Gesù nel Fratello
by Hugh J. Moran
Printed in Hong Kong
Library of Congress Catalog Number: 79-88680
ISBN 0-911782-34-6

Scripture quotations are from the Revised Standard Version of
the Bible, copyrighted 1946, 1952 © 1971, 1973. Used
with permission.

Quotations from Council Documents are from *The Documents
of Vatican II,* edited by W.M. Abbott, reprinted with permission
of America Press, Inc., 106 W. 56 St., New York, N.Y. 10019,
© 1966. All rights reserved.

Nihil Obstat: Charles E. Diviney, P.A.
                Diocesan Censor
Imprimatur: Francis J. Mugavero, D.D.
               Bishop of Brooklyn
Brooklyn, N.Y. June 27, 1979

1st Printing 1979
2nd Printing 1980

CONTENTS

FOREWORD

I find it a joy when familiar words and phrases suddenly sound strangely new, when the meaning of simple sayings rings deeply again in the soul. Such has been my experience in reading these marvelous talks given by Chiara Lubich, foundress and President of the Focolare Movement. These simple words of faith invite us to enter upon a divine adventure,—to rediscover the profound power of the Gospel, to thrill to the love of God all about us, to marvel at the presence of Jesus in our brothers and sisters.

Jesus confounded, even embarrassed, the scribes and the Pharisees with the simplicity of His message. Imagine,—the whole law and the prophets contained simply in our love of God and our love of neighbor. This love creates unity, and unity, in turn, promotes love in a catalytic embrace. It is the charism of Chiara that such transcendent themes come through these pages so simply, so clearly, so engagingly.

As one who is in love and on fire with the Word of God in her heart, Chiara makes it utterly believable that the human person, whoever and wherever, is utterly lovable. This is the source of the faith and enthusiasm which Chiara shares with us so beautifully in these precious words.

† John Cardinal Cody
Archbishop of Chicago

1

Made in God's image

In the course of this book I intend to consider in depth the true nature of that extraordinary being, the human being. I hope to bring out the riches that are to be found in every human being, and to discover God's plan for each person we meet, as this affects his or her relationship with each one of us.

The experience of our Movement

Our movement has always had an enormous respect for every human being. From the very beginning, we used to say with great conviction that we cannot go to God alone, but we must go to him with our brothers and sisters, since he is the Father of us all.

Initially, in our special concern for the poor (though without overlooking others), and later, in our contact with everyone, we discovered how much each person enriched our lives; and we realized that, in the Movement, after God, for God, and with God, our neighbor has first place.

The fact is that the Movement has always tried to live the essence of the Christian message. For this reason, when someone asks what the basic teachings of the Movement are, we respond with the same words Jesus used in answering the Pharisees: "You shall love the Lord your God with all your heart, and with all your soul, and with all your mind.... You shall love your neighbor as yourself" (Mt. 22:37-39).

It is through our neighbor that we continually pass from an empty and meaningless life to a full life: "We have passed out of death into life, because we love the brethren" (1 Jn. 3:14).

When we love our neighbor, we notice that our union with God grows.

With our neighbor we can already begin here on earth to pattern our lives on the life of the Trinity; we can erect a temple of God in the midst of the world; and we can experience a foretaste of heaven in this life.

In the Movement we do not use extraordinary means of mortification because in loving our neighbor and making ourselves one with him or her—which requires the silence or death of our own ego—we have found a way to demolish our old self and allow our new self to live.

All this is possible because in one way or another, Christ renders himself present in every human being: in everyone we meet, we meet the Lord.

Anyone who observes the life of the Movement from without, can clearly see how this aspect is understood and lived. Recently, for example, a prominent Catholic remarked that in our spirituality we take our neighbor "incredibly seriously." In the Movement, he said, one does not only find that attitude of human solidarity which is so stressed in the various secular and Marxist humanisms of our day; nor does one merely encounter a fraternal solidarity based on our "common destiny" (currently a much-used expression in several parts of the world). No. The Movement, he continued, has emphasized that each of our fellow human beings is not merely a relative or a co-worker, a companion in joy or someone entrusted to our care, and still less a rival in battle. Every person is an individual loved by Jesus, and in whom Jesus—who is always present, though in different ways in different persons— must take shape. In each person I meet, Jesus comes to me: as a gift, an enrichment, an encouragement, a purification; and in each person, Jesus wants to be loved and served.

The anthropological trend in theology, he continued, has centered its attention on the human person utilizing the findings of modern psychology, sociology and education, which ought not to be underestimated. These theological efforts have certainly produced valuable contributions, but in the final analysis, he said, it is revelation which must determine anthropology.

He concluded by saying that the Movement also focuses its attention on the human person but in the right way: according to revelation.

The members of the Movement, with God's grace, continually try to love those around them, even in the most insignificant circumstances of life. Whenever they forget to do so, they begin again, with that complete concern for the other's needs which is the best antidote for egoism. They show by their actions that love of neighbor is not an unattainable ideal—provided that one desires to relive the life of Jesus today. As a consequence, since the flame of this supernatural love is difficult to resist, it has grown into a blazing fire.

We went out to love our brothers and sisters first in Trent, then throughout Italy, Europe, and the world. From person to person, a vast network of love was spread over the earth among people of all ages, vocations, and social backgrounds.

And with ever-increasing intensity we continued, keeping up as much as possible with what was happening everywhere else in the world, and—on a more intimate level—sharing the sufferings that cause Jesus to grow in each one of us: all for one, and one for all.

Beginning in 1960, God put us in contact not only with our fellow Catholics, but with our Christian brothers and sisters in other Churches and denominations. And since 1976, we have come into more direct contact with our brothers and sisters of other religions, or—to speak more generically—with those who do not know Jesus.

We did not stop in the face of this more difficult responsibility, because God's grace quickly spurred us on to a sincere and enthusiastic love for these immense portions of humanity.

I recently heard someone refer to this aspect of the Work of Mary as a continuation of the episode of the Visitation, in which Mary sets out "with haste" to visit Elizabeth, in spite of the distance which separates them. She who was full of grace set out to visit her cousin, bearing Jesus in her womb. She was also bringing Jesus to the one who was to be his precursor, in order that he might be sanctified. But in bringing Jesus, Mary understood even more profoundly the mystery that had been entrusted to her, and she expressed it in the "Magnificat" (Lk. 1:46-55).

The Movement offers itself—and this is the life style of the entire Church—so that it might become a means of encounter between Jesus and his present-day precursors, so to speak; that is, between Jesus in Christians and those "seeds of the Word" which are present in the believers of the various other religions. Like the Church, the Movement also wants to be a means of encounter between Jesus and the hearts and minds of those who reject God, but who—because they are made in his image, and because the human soul is naturally Christian—still tend unconsciously toward this meeting with the Lord.

As the members of the Movement hasten toward these new brothers and sisters, a new light is enkindled in their minds, and they realize the greatness of the vocation to which the Movement has been called. And in their hearts they utter a small "Magnificat."

But who are these persons whom we have rushed out to meet, or whom we desire to encounter?

If we look at the words of Scripture we will find an answer, and we will understand more deeply what the Holy Spirit has been, and still is, prompting us to do.

The Old Testament view

Let us go back to the book of Genesis: "Then God said, 'Let us make man in our image, after our likeness....' So God created man in his own image" (Gen. 1:26-27). This passage does not so much tell us what a human being is, as what God intended to do and did; that is, it tells us who we are according to God's creative purpose. The decision to create humankind and its actual creation in God's image are tightly bound to one another. These words of Genesis tell us that the Creator set out to create someone who would have a relationship with him.

Unlike all other created beings, including the animals, which Genesis says were created "according to their kinds" (Gen. 1:25), only Man is created "in the image of God" (Gen. 1:27). Human beings, therefore, are the only creatures who have a direct, personal relationship with God: they stand before him, his "you." This special relationship with God is what constitutes being human. "The relationship with God is not something added to human nature, rather Man is created such that his human nature is understood within his relationship with God."[1]

This is stupendous! And it is true! Does not humankind itself "call for" the existence of God, thereby becoming the greatest witness to God's existence? Do not human beings alone—in contrast to all the other beings on earth—feel in their hearts a desire for something or someone transcendent, and a longing for what is infinite and immortal?

And when they fail to find a solution to the innumerable problems that the universe presents, do they not lift their gaze in search of Someone who must be there because he cannot *not* be there? Yes, this is how human beings act when they are pure and sincere.

Moreover, if human life only has meaning in the context of a relationship with God, then religion is not just one aspect of life; rather, it must involve the whole of it.

Thank you, God, for the Ideal you have given us! For that is what you have taught us: that religion must involve everything else.

For people in today's world, this is a revolution. But you have told us that the twenty-four hours of every day must be for you. You are the one who wants our whole heart, our whole mind, our whole strength. And even when we are loving or thinking about or doing something for someone other than you, it is still for you and in you that we must love, think, and act.

"God said, 'Let us make man in our image, after our likeness' " (Gen. 1:26). Commenting on this passage, Irenaeus, bishop of Lyons, wrote:

> Angels had no power to make an image of God, nor [did] anyone else.... God did not stand in need of these beings in order to accomplish what He had Himself determined...should be done.... For with Him were always present...

the Son and the Spirit...to whom He speaks, saying, "Let us make man after our image and likeness" (Gen. 1:26).[2]

How true this interpretation seems to me! For when God created Man, he created humankind as a whole, as "someone" who stands before him. And if humanity wishes to be as God wants it to be, it must be in the image of God, who is one and triune. Human beings must live in a relationship of love with one another as do the persons of the Trinity, in whose image they have been created.

Furthermore, if in creating Man, God created all people and placed them in this relationship with him, then each and every person is called to this relationship regardless of the diversity in human nature, regardless of differences in religious belief, and regardless of whether one is a believer or not.

The Second Vatican Council also interprets the passage, "in the image of God he created him; male and female he created them" (Gen. 1:27), as meaning that to be made in God's image involves a special relationship with God: human beings have the capacity to know and love God. This is true not only in the sense that, since each human person is made in God's likeness, he or she is capable of having a rapport with him, but in an even stronger sense: human beings are capable of knowing and

19

loving like God—God, the only being whose very nature is to know and to love.

Gregory of Nyssa affirms: "God is also love and the source of love. . . . the Creator has made this our characteristic as well. . . . Therefore, if love is lacking, the entire character of the image is altered."[3]

John Chrysostom tells us how this image is to be treated:

> How many men have not only cast down, but also trodden underfoot the images of God! For when you throttle a debtor, when you strip him, when you drag him away, you trample underfoot God's image. . . . But if you say that man is not of the same substance as God—what does that matter? . . . If men are not of the same substance as God, . . . still they have been called His image; and it is fitting they should receive honor on that account.[4]

Sin has not caused this image to be destroyed or lost. Origen declares: "The image of God remains in you always, even though you cover it over with the image of the earthly man."[5]

However, even though it has not been destroyed by sin, it has been disfigured. Thus we have the coming of Jesus, who restores us to God's image.

Augustine says: "Man was made in God's image and likeness, and he defaced it by sin. His true and lasting good therefore will be assured if this [image] is stamped anew [by Baptism]."[6]

Irenaeus affirms that it is necessary to be "grafted" into the Word of God in order to live in the image and likeness of God.

> St. Paul says, "But you, being a wild olive-tree, have been grafted into the good olive-tree, and have been made a partaker of the richness of the olive-tree" (Rom. 11:17,24).... [In the same way,] those persons who are not bringing forth the fruits of righteousness, and are, as it were, covered over and lost among brambles, if they use diligence and receive the word of God as a graft, arrive at the original nature of man—that which was created after the image and likeness of God."[7]

Finally, Paul VI sees in Mary "... the woman, the true woman who is ideal and real, the person in whom the image of God is reflected with absolute clarity."[8] And he urges Christians to imitate her:

> It is impossible to honor her who is "full of grace" (Lk. 1:28) without thereby honoring in oneself the state of grace, which is friendship with God, communion with him, and the

21

indwelling of the Holy Spirit. It is this divine grace which takes possession of the whole man and conforms him to the image of the Son of God.... Mary, the New Woman, stands at the side of Christ, the New Man, within whose mystery alone, the mystery of man finds true light.[9]

Persons created by God

Although the Old Testament expresses the greatness and dignity of human nature by revealing that human beings are made in God's image, nonetheless, it stresses above all that they are created, created by God.

Therefore, insofar as they are created, their being is radically different from that of their Creator, and they are totally dependent on him for their existence. "A living relationship with God is always essential to full human existence. The godless man is considered lost...perverted in his very being."[10]

Persons to be loved

In the Old Testament human beings are presented as persons who are to be treated with love. In Leviticus, God commands:

You shall not hate your brother in your heart, but you shall reason with your neighbor, lest you bear sin because of him. You shall not take vengeance or bear any grudge against the sons of your own people, but you shall love your neighbor as yourself: I am the Lord. . . .

The stranger who sojourns with you shall be to you as the native among you, and you shall love him as yourself; for you were strangers in the land of Egypt (Lev. 19:17-18, 34).

Worship, ritual, and the prophets

Worship and ritual were desired and established by God, as described elsewhere in Leviticus. But when the Jewish people believed they were satisfying him by simply performing the prescribed rites, then God sent the prophets who called them back to an interior conversion that was to be expressed in love of one's neighbor as a witness of one's love for God. For we can see that whenever God's law was scorned in human relationships, and God himself was sought after only in ritual forms of worship, then God was reduced to "an impersonal source of magical power, which can be manipulated with no feeling of reverence whatsoever simply by means of a meticulous routine."[11]

When they saw that by means of such rituals religion was being falsified at its very heart, the

23

prophets had no choice but to repudiate these ritual observances, which had aroused God's judgment and indignation:

I hate, I despise your feasts, and I take no delight in your solemn assemblies. Even though you offer me your burnt offerings...I will not accept them.... Take away from me the noise of your songs; to the melody of your harps I will not listen. But let justice roll down like water, and righteousness like an ever-flowing stream (Amos 5:21-24).

...the Lord has a controversy with the inhabitants of the land. There is no faithfulness or kindness...there is swearing, lying, killing, stealing, and committing adultery; they break all bounds and murder follows murder. Therefore the land mourns, and all who dwell in it languish (Hos. 4:1-3).

For I desire steadfast love and not sacrifice, the knowledge of God, rather than burnt offerings (Hos. 6:6).

When you spread forth your hands, I will hide my eyes from you; even though you make many prayers, I will not listen.... Learn to do good; seek justice, correct oppression; defend the fatherless, plead for the widow (Is. 1:15,17).

This controversy concerning worship and ritual shows that "the right relationship with God is determined by means of the right relationship with our fellow human beings and that the service of the divine liturgy must always be accompanied by the service of our fellow men and women."[12]

In the final analysis, what the prophets were actually coming out so strongly against was "a perversion of meaning which has threatened all human worship through the centuries: sacrifice, worship, and prayer only keep their true sense as long as in them men are really concerned to encounter the holy God. If man tries to make use of them to give himself security in the sight of God, then they become a blasphemy; sacrifice becomes a means of self-justification, the celebration of feasts the occasion of mere emotional exaltation, and prayer a meaningless, craven, or hypocritical wailing."[13]

The fasting which pleases God: love of neighbor

God does not even like the observance of fasting when it is not linked to love for one's neighbor, as he shows in Isaiah:

> Cry aloud, spare not, lift up your voice like a trumpet; declare to my people their transgression.... Behold, you fast only to quarrel and to

fight and to hit with wicked fist. Fasting like yours this day will not make your voice to be heard on high. Is such the fast that I choose, a day for a man to humble himself? Is it to bow his head like a rush, and to spread sackcloth and ashes under him? Will you call this a fast, and a day acceptable to the Lord?

Is not this the fast that I choose: to loose the bonds of wickedness, to undo the thongs of the yoke, to let the oppressed go free, and to break every yoke? Is it not to share your bread with the hungry, and bring the homeless poor into your house; when you see the naked, to cover him, and not to hide yourself from your own flesh? . . . Then you shall call, and the Lord will answer; you shall cry, and he will say, Here I am (Is. 58:1, 4-7, 9; see also Is. 59).

After such a severe criticism of the abuse of fast days, one would expect the rites themselves to be confirmed as being holy. Yet the opposite occurs. Though not questioning the practice of fast days as such, the prophet radically challenges the accompanying practices (humbling oneself, bowing one's head, using sackcloth and ashes, etc.). The fasting which pleases God consists in replacing actions directed towards God with actions directed towards one's neighbor. In so doing, one is truly mortifying oneself, and offering God another kind of fasting.

Among the various acts of this sort, one is particularly pleasing to God: loosing the bonds of injustice and freeing the oppressed. The experience of exile and slavery in Egypt, followed by the experience of being liberated by God, had given Israel a new appreciation of the meaning of freedom.

The other acts listed by the prophet are the traditional acts of assistance to those in need. We are presented with a panorama of those least-regarded by society: the poor, the outcasts, slaves, prisoners, the hungry, the homeless, those dressed in rags. The picture is similar to that of the Last Judgment (see Mt. 25:35-36). God says to come to their assistance "and not to hide yourself [pretending not to notice (see Dt. 22:1)] from your own flesh" (Is. 58:7); that is, from your own flesh and blood, which can be interpreted as referring to every human being, and not merely one's fellow countrymen—which was the general interpretation among the Jews (see Job 31:15).[14]

How beautiful are these words of Job:

I delivered the poor who cried,
    and the fatherless who had none to help him.
The blessing of him who was about to perish
    came upon me,

27

and I caused the widow's heart to sing for
joy. . . .
I was eyes to the blind,
    and feet to the lame.
I was a father to the poor,
    and I searched out the cause of him whom I did
    not know.

(Job 29:12-13, 15-16)

If we perform the deeds which constitute a "fast"
acceptable to the Lord, then we will experience
blessings.

Love for enemies

Lastly, the Old Testament is not lacking in
references to loving one's enemies: "If your enemy
is hungry, give him bread to eat; and if he is thirsty
give him water to drink; for you will heap coals of
fire on his head, and the Lord will reward you"
(Pr. 25:21-22; see also Sir. 28:1-9).

2

Jesus' presence in the Christian
as presented in the New Testament

If we read through the New Testament—particularly the four Gospels, the letters of Paul, and the First Letter of John—we find clear and frequently stupendous affirmations of the presence of Jesus in our neighbor.

The Gospels

Let us begin with the Gospels. In some passages Jesus identifies himself with the apostles or with those he has sent out; in others, with his followers; and in still others, with every human being. This identification can be understood from the contexts in which Jesus is speaking.

Jesus present in the apostles

Jesus' presence in his apostles is affirmed in all four Gospels, with illustrations that range from giving them a welcome that is more than mere hospitality, to listening to them. For example:

He who receives you receives me, and he who receives me receives him who sent me (Mt. 10:40).

He who hears you hears me, and he who rejects you rejects me, and he who rejects me rejects him who sent me (Lk. 10:16).

Truly, truly, I say to you, he who receives anyone whom I send receives me; and he who receives me receives him who sent me (Jn. 13:20).

In this missionary context, Jesus also identifies himself with a "child" and with "little ones" (Mk. 9:37; Mt. 10:42), but it is probable that these words are also meant to indicate those he is sending out. For among those sent out by Jesus there were some who did not enjoy the esteem of the people; in fact, they might even have been treated with contempt. So Jesus speaks out in their behalf. He wants to inspire love for them in the Christian communities, and he wants his followers to do the same. For however weak or mediocre his messengers may be, they bring his word. In the Old Testament, in fact, the messenger was considered the mouth of the one who had sent him (see Jer. 15:19); and according to Jewish tradition the emissary *(shaliah)* of a man is like the man himself.

We can presume, therefore, that in using the words which have come down to us as "child" in

Mark and "little ones" in Matthew, Jesus was referring to those he was sending out as his emissaries:

> Whoever receives one such child in my name receives me; and whoever receives me, receives not me but him who sent me (Mk. 9:37).
> And whoever gives to one of these little ones even a cup of cold water because he is a disciple, truly, I say to you, he shall not lose his reward (Mt. 10:42).

This presence of Jesus in his apostles, in those he has sent as his emissaries, receives a new value after his death and resurrection. For after the resurrection, the apostles are incorporated into Christ, and he is actually mystically present in them. Their word is then efficacious of itself, and not only because they have been charged with passing it on. Jesus is acting in them; therefore whoever receives one of the apostles after Jesus' resurrection experiences a real encounter with him. Paul, too, stresses this on various occasions:

> You received me as an angel of God, as Christ Jesus (Gal. 4:14).
> When you received the word of God which you heard from us, you accepted it not as the word of

men but as what it really is, the word of God, which is at work in you believers (1 Thess. 2:13).

So we are ambassadors for Christ, God making his appeal through us (2 Cor. 5:20). You desire proof that Christ is speaking in me (2 Cor. 13:3).

Jesus present in the disciples

The Gospels also give us affirmations of the presence of Jesus in the ordinary Christian, in the context of the life of the community formed by his disciples. Words such as "who receives you, receives me," originally referring only to those sent out by Jesus, are later generalized and applied to the relationships between the members of the Christian community, particularly with regard to those in need. Love directed toward the least and the neediest of one's brothers and sisters must be considered as love for Jesus in person. For example Luke relates this episode:

And an argument arose among them as to which of them was the greatest. But when Jesus perceived the thought of their hearts, he took a child and put him by his side, and said to them, "Whoever receives this child in my name receives him who sent me; for he who is least among you all is the one who is great" (Lk. 9:46-48).

34

In this instance, as in so many others, Jesus completely overturns the normal scale of values: that which other people treat with contempt, he puts in a position of prominence. As a consequence, for Christians, the poorest and the least are in reality the greatest and the most important, because Jesus has put himself on their side—so much so, that whoever receives one such person receives Jesus himself.[1]

We are dealing here with relationships between Christians, wherein the motivation for loving is consciously supernatural. For Jesus says that the person must be received "in my name": with full knowledge, therefore, of what one is doing, and with the intention of following the Lord's teaching. Jesus' entire life is an extraordinary and wonderful lesson on how to treat those in need.

Jesus' solidarity with all his followers without distinction, but particularly with those who are suffering, is also expressed in the words addressed to Saul outside Damascus, as he was heading there to arrest the Christians: " 'Saul, Saul, why do you persecute me?' And he said, 'Who are you, Lord?' And he said, 'I am Jesus, whom you are persecuting' " (Acts 9:4-5).

Jesus present in every person

In the Gospels we also find affirmations of the

presence of Jesus in every human being. We need only call to mind the cosmic vision of the Last Judgment, which concludes with the affirmation: "...as you did it to one of the least of these my brethren, you did it to me" (Mt. 25:40). But we will consider this presence of Jesus in a later chapter.

The letters of Paul

Jesus' presence in those who believe

Let us now look at what Paul's letters have to say about the presence of Christ in the Christian. Rather than speak of Christ in the believer, Paul generally prefers another expression: to be "in Christ," by which he wants to indicate the believer's incorporation into Christ's body, the Church, which has taken place at Baptism. This expression occurs one hundred and sixty-four times in his letters.

This reality of unity, this communitarian aspect brought out by our being "in Christ," is also expressed with the words "Christ in": "Here there cannot be Greek and Jew,...slave, free man, but Christ is all, and in all" (Col. 3:11). What Paul is emphasizing here is that Christ, who is present in each of us, has made us all members of his Body. Since Christ has placed us in this unity, which is himself, we are all brothers and sisters, irrespective of all previous differences of race, nationality, social standing, etc.

This being "in Christ" simultaneously brings about a personal unity between the Christian and Jesus, a union so profound that it creates in the Christian a new "self." For Paul, in fact, the presence of Jesus in the believer is a mystical identification: the believer becomes one being with Christ. ("Identification" here signifies a very profound union, which has no parallel on the natural-human level; a union, however, in which the distinction between the persons is preserved.)

When Paul affirms, "It is no longer I who live, but Christ who lives in me" (Gal. 2:20), he is not speaking merely of a mystical experience he has had, but of that identification of the believer with Christ which is the totally new thing about being a Christian, and which has made him a new person.

This indwelling of Christ in the believer gives rise to a marvelous consequence: Christians need no longer be anxious about seeking self-fulfillment or planning out their future. They have only to adhere to Christ living in them, who will then gradually reveal his plan for each individual and will guide him or her through a great divine adventure, hitherto unknown.

This is what all the members of the Movement have set out to do, once they have discovered its particular charism, which, seen in this light, is nothing other than a new understanding of Christianity—new, because it has been revived by the Spirit.

The believer "with" Christ

This identification of the Christian with Jesus certainly does not mean that the believer is absorbed by him. What it implies is a communion of life, and therefore dialogue, dynamism, growth, "until"—as Paul says—"Christ be formed in you" (Gal. 4:19).

In order to express this mysterious sharing in the life of Jesus, Paul uses the expression "to be with Christ." In fact, he coins new verbs with the Greek prefix *syn* ("with," "together") in order to show that the Christian's life conforms to the life of Christ: it is an experience of death and resurrection.

> You were *buried with him* in baptism, in which you were also *raised with him* . . . (Col. 2:12).
> Our old self was *crucified with him* . . . (Rom. 6:6).
> If we *have died with him*, we shall also *live with him* (2 Tim. 2:11).
> . . . we *have been united with him* in a death like his . . . (Rom. 6:5).
> God . . . made us *alive together with Christ* . . . (Eph. 2:4-5).

From this perspective as well, we have seen that the life of the members of the Movement as a whole retraces the footsteps of Jesus: in his joy and his suffering, his successes and his abandonment, and in that glory which is compatible with our earthly life.

The bond between Christianity and the New Covenant

We could cite many other passages of Paul regarding the presence of Jesus in the believer. However, I would now like to focus on the way Paul frequently connects the reality brought by Jesus with the great promise of the Spirit's presence in human hearts (Rom. 8; 1 Thess. 4:9), which we find in Jeremiah and Ezekiel as a characteristic of the New Covenant:

> But this is the covenant which I will make with the house of Israel after those days, says the Lord: I will put my law within them, and I will write it upon their hearts; and I will be their God, and they shall be my people. And no longer shall each man teach his neighbor . . . for they shall all know me, from the least of them to the greatest, says the Lord (Jer. 31:33-34).

Ezekiel identifies the law written in their hearts, which Jeremiah speaks of, with the very Spirit of God: "And I will put my spirit within you, and cause you to walk in my statutes and be careful to observe my ordinances" (Ez. 36:27).

Precisely because of this indwelling of God in the Christian, he or she is no longer obeying or disobeying a commandment, even one which is God-given, but is either submitting to or directly opposing "God's activity in the very heart of the Christian through the gift of His Spirit."[2]

Paul sees all this fulfilled in the Christian community: "But concerning love of the brethren you have no need to have any one write to you, for you yourselves have been taught by God to love one another" (1 Thess. 4:9).

Therefore, the presence of Christ in the heart of the believer by means of the Spirit is the accomplishment of the definitive, eschatological presence of God in humanity and in the Church.

The relationship and the difference between the presence of Jesus and the presence of the Holy Spirit

The presence of the Spirit in the Christian and the presence of Jesus in the Christian are inseparably bound to one another. To have the Spirit signifies that one belongs to Christ. Christ gives himself to the believer in the Spirit.

The theologian Durrwell shows the difference between these two presences very well:

Christ is present in the faithful. Also, "God has sent the Spirit of his Son into your hearts" (Gal. 4:6). But each of these guests is established in us in his own fashion.... Whereas the Spirit is *given* to us,...we *are* the body of Christ. Whereas our bodies are the temple of the Spirit, they are the members of Christ (1 Cor. 6:15,19). The Spirit dwells in Christ and in us who are the body of Christ. The guest is not confused with the house in which he dwells. Though filling all things, the Spirit does not identify the faithful with himself.[3]

But Christ does.

Jesus in the believer according to John

John, like Paul, has his own way of speaking about the presence of Jesus in the Christian. His characteristic formula is: the believer in Christ, and Christ in the believer. For John, therefore, this indwelling is mutual.

In his Gospel he speaks of it with reference to the Eucharist: "He who eats my flesh and drinks my blood abides in me and I in him" (Jn. 6:56). The word "abide" is consoling because it gives the idea of a mutual immanence that is not momentary, but

41

permanent. Therefore, we can be in union with Christ the whole day long. And this union is a profound interpenetration which has no parallel on the human level.

John speaks of this immanence again when he gives the very appropriate example of the vine and the branches: "I am the vine, you are the branches. He who abides in me, and I in him...bears much fruit, for apart from me you can do nothing.... If you abide in me, and my words abide in you, ask whatever you will, and it shall be done for you" (15:5,7).

And he speaks of it again in the seventeenth chapter where he says, for example, "I in them and you in me, that they may become perfectly one..." (verse 23).

John does not speak only of the presence of Christ in the believer; but he states explicitly that the Trinity itself comes to dwell in the Christian. Let us look, for example, at Chapter 14:15-23.

The first part deals with the presence of the Holy Spirit in the believers. His coming is linked to the departure of Jesus, and his role is to render Jesus present in them. Before Jesus' death, in fact, his disciples remained outside of him, so to speak. But after the Resurrection, the action of the Holy Spirit brings about the presence of the glorified Christ within the believer. From this comes the new relationship of the believer with Jesus:

I will pray the Father, and he will give you
another Counselor, to be with you forever, the
Spirit of truth, whom the world cannot receive,
because it neither sees him nor knows him; you
know him, for he dwells with you, and will be in
you (14:16-17).

In the second part, John says that it is a characteristic of the risen Christ to be with the Father, and
that through Christ the believer can also be with the
Father, in a new relationship with him:

I will not leave you desolate; I will come to
you. . . . In that day you will know that I am in the
Father, and you in me, and I in you (14:18,20).

In the third part we find the condition set by Jesus
for his presence in the believer: faithfulness to his
commandments, which leads to a deeper understanding of God. If this condition is met, the Trinity
will come to dwell in the believer:

He who has my commandments and keeps
them, he it is who loves me; and he who loves me
will be loved by my father, and I will love him and
manifest myself to him. . . . If a man loves me, he
will keep my word, and my Father will love him,
and we will come to him and make our home with
him (14:21,23).

43

M.J. Lagrange comments on this moving final verse:

> Nothing is demanded by way of intellectual culture, tendency toward contemplation, or some special asceticism.... God does not come to call forth ecstasy or any other outward manifestation. He comes to dwell in the heart of the one who loves him. Nothing could be simpler as an expression of this mysticism, and nothing could be more profound.[4]

John not only affirms this mutual indwelling in his Gospel, but also in his first letter—but with a variation: instead of speaking of Jesus he speaks of God (see 1 Jn. 3:24). The content does not change, however, because the presence of God implies the presence of Christ, and in this letter John asserts in a unique way that Jesus Christ is God.

He also reiterates and clarifies the condition under which God remains in us and we in God: that we keep God's commandments. And these he reduces to two: believe in Jesus, and love one another (see 1 Jn. 3:23).

Furthermore, he states that the Spirit who moves us to confess our faith in Jesus and to love each other is the same Spirit who guarantees that God lives in us (see 1 Jn. 3:23-24).

At this point I cannot go on without giving special thanks to God. Everyone who knows the Movement's history knows that at the beginning the first Focolarine[5] decided to live the New Commandment, and that all who have begun to live this spirituality since then have made the same decision. Now John explains who it was who urged us to choose that particular commandment, and instilled in our hearts such a great faith in the Gospel. It was the Holy Spirit. Let us give him thanks forever.

And another joyous observation: if we believed and if we loved one another, then Christ was in us and we in him. May he always keep it this way!

Now allow me to conclude this brief examination of the presence of God (or Christ) in the believer, by turning to the revelation central to Christianity: God is love.

John says that "God is love, and he who abides in love abides in God, and God abides in him" (1 Jn. 4:16), because love, reciprocal love, which presupposes faith, is the condition for remaining in communion with God.

And God who is Love is the immense sun which has enlightened and continues to enlighten all those who encounter the Movement. God who is Love: for us—as for others—he was, is, and will always be the starting point and foundation of our entire

Christian life.

And finally, here is a verse from the book of Revelation (the Apocalypse), also the work of John, which beautifully shows again that God is love and that, as such, he dwells in us. These words should fill our hearts with joy: "Behold, I stand at the door and knock; if any one hears my voice and opens the door, I will come in to him and eat with him, and he with me" (Rev. 3:20). To eat with Jesus: yes, for when one experiences the profound happiness of that intimate conversation with God, it is like sharing a banquet of love with him.

3
Jesus in those who suffer

The Last Judgment

I think it is appropriate to read now, in its entirety, the passage describing the most awe-inspiring and momentous event that all of us will one day have to experience:

When the Son of man comes in his glory, and all the angels with him, then he will sit on his glorious throne. Before him will be gathered all the nations, and he will separate them one from another as a shepherd separates the sheep from the goats, and he will place the sheep at his right hand, but the goats at the left. Then the King will say to those at his right hand, "Come, O blessed of my Father, inherit the kingdom prepared for you from the foundation of the world; for I was hungry and you gave me food, I was thirsty and you gave me drink, I was a stranger and you welcomed me, I was naked and you clothed me, I was sick and you visited me, I was in prison and you came to me." Then the righteous will answer him, "Lord, when did we see you hungry and feed you, or thirsty and give you drink? And when did we see you a stranger and welcome you, or naked and clothe you? And when did we see you sick or in prison and visit you?" And the King will answer them, "Truly, I say to you, as you did it to one of the least of these my brethren, you did it to me." Then he will say to those at his left hand, "Depart from me, you cursed, into the eternal fire prepared for the devil and his angels; for I was hungry and you gave me no food, I was thirsty and you gave me no drink, I was a stranger and you did not welcome me, naked and you did not clothe me, sick and in prison and you did not visit me." Then they also will answer, "Lord, when did we see you hungry or thirsty or a stranger or naked or sick or in prison, and did not minister to you?" Then he will answer them, "Truly, I say to you, as you did it not to one of the least of these, you did it not to me." And they will go away into eternal punishment, but the righteous into eternal life" (Mt. 25:31-46).

Here we see the importance of every neighbor, especially those in need. *We* are the ones who need *them* in order to possess eternal life; and if we do not care for them, we cannot escape hell.

50

Jesus in the needy according to the Fathers of the Church

John Chrysostom tried to open the eyes of the Christians of his day to this truth, which at once inspires fear and joy, and which then, as now, Christians often forgot:

> But we...do not even feed [the poor man] when he is hungry.... And yet if you saw Christ himself, every one of you would strip himself of all his possessions. But even now it is [Christ], for he himself has said, "It is I." Why then do you not strip yourself of everything? For even now you hear him say, "you do it to me.".... In fact, if he were not the one to receive what you give, he would not grant you the kingdom. If you were not rejecting [Christ] himself, when you despise him in any person, he would not send you to hell. But it is precisely because you are despising him, that the blame is so great.[1]

Thinking this over carefully, it seems that of all God has commanded us to do, one thing alone is of value: love for the suffering and for those in need. It is "as if," in the words of Leo the Great, "those on the right had no other virtue, and those on the left no other sin."[2]

51

In reading the Fathers of the Church, I found fiery words that reinforce this truth. The unexcelled master on the subject is the enlightened and forceful John Chrysostom.

The following passage in his *Homilies on the Gospel of Matthew* made my heart jump for joy, because it seems to me that the Lord has always directed us to focus our attention first of all on our neighbor whom we see, in order to love concretely God whom we do not see—just as the apostle John tells us (see 1 Jn. 4:20). Then everything else becomes worthwhile, including the liturgy and every form of worship. "So if...your brother has something against you, leave your gift there before the altar and go; first be reconciled to your brother" (Mt. 5:23-24). "Above all, hold unfailing your love for one another" (1 Pet. 4:8).

Here, then, are the eloquent words of John Chrysostom:

What does Christ gain if his table [altar] is covered with cups of gold, while he himself is dying of hunger in those who are poor? First fill him in his hunger, and then decorate his altar. Will you offer him a golden chalice and not give him a glass of cold water? What good will that do him? You obtain cloths woven with gold for the altar, but you do not offer him the clothes he

52

needs.... Tell me: if you were to see a man without sufficient food, would you leave him in his hunger and set about covering the table with silver? Do you think he would thank you, or would he not instead become indignant? And if you were to see someone dressed in rags, and not bother to give him something to wear; but instead, you began to erect gilded columns, saying that you were doing it in his honor, don't you think he would consider that you were mocking him, and that what you were doing was an insult of the worst kind? Then think the same way with regard to Christ when he is going about as a wanderer or a stranger in need of a roof to shelter him.... I say this not to prohibit you from honoring him with such gifts, but to exhort you to help the poor as well as give gifts, or rather, to help the poor before giving gifts.

God has never blamed anyone for not having given expensive gifts to adorn his temples; but as regards not helping the poor, he threatens us with hell. Therefore, while adorning his house, do not overlook your brother who is in distress, for he is more properly a temple than the [church building is].

These treasures of yours [in the churches] can be despoiled by unbelieving kings, tyrants, and thieves, but what you have done for your brother who is hungry or a stranger or naked, not even the devil can take from you because it will be laid up in a safe place.[3]

And Cyprian was of the same mind:

With your patrimony...feed Christ.... Lay up your treasures where no thief will dig them up and no treacherous robber will break in. Acquire possessions for yourself, but in heaven, where your fruits will last for all eternity, free from every contact with the world's injustice, and where no rust will consume them, where no hail can strike them down, where the sun will not burn them nor the rain ruin them. For you are offending God himself if you believe that he has given you wealth so that you could make use of it without concern for salvation.[4]

Love for the poor becomes a source of great peace and hope when we realize that, since Jesus considers as done to him whatever we do for those in need, he becomes indebted to us and we become his creditors. Ambrose affirms this:

Lend the Lord your money through the hands of the poor. The Lord is held liable; he records whatever the needy man receives. The gospel is your guarantee.... Why do you hesitate to give?... For you, the poor man is the Lord of heaven and the Creator of this world. Are you still trying to think how you can find a richer guarantor?[5]

Gifts given to the poor put God under obligation, for it is written, "Whoever gives to the poor lends to the Lord" (Prov. 19:17).[6]

And Augustine says that the recompense we will receive from Jesus will be great:

Listen to what you will receive in possessions from him to whom you have made your loan: "Come, O blessed of my Father, inherit...." Desire this, work to obtain this, let this be the purpose of your lending.[7]

Jesus in the needy according to the saints

The Curé of Ars once made a statement that shows how the supernatural (and thus true) way of looking at things was almost second nature to him: "Frequently we believe we are giving assistance to a poor person, and in reality it turns out to be the Lord."[8]

On another occasion, he cleared up a doubt that

all of us can have when it comes to helping someone unknown:

> There are those who say: "Oh, he will make bad use of it." Let him do what he wants with it. The poor person will be judged on what use he or she made of your gift, and you will be judged on the basis of the gift you could have given and did not give.[9]

The fact is that the saints have always been great experts in loving those who suffer and leaders in establishing all sorts of initiatives and institutions to help them. But above all they have shown themselves to be human beings with hearts. For instance, they say that St. Francis "seemed to have a mother's heart."[10] The saints are persons who have felt the sufferings of the poor and the needy as their own, and have loved Christ in them to such an extent that Our Lord did not wait for the next life in order to show himself to them, as we read of Catherine of Siena:

> She was accosted by a beggar, who asked her, for the love of God, to help him in his need. Not having anything to give him, she told him to wait until she had got home. But the beggar persisted: "If you have anything to give me, give it to me

now, because the truth is I'm desperate."

Not wishing to send him away disappointed, she wondered what she could give him, and then she remembered a little silver cross that hung at the end of her beads. She quickly broke the thread and gave the beggar the cross. As soon as he had been given it he went off perfectly content without asking anyone else for anything.

During the night, while the virgin of the Lord was as usual at prayer, the Savior of the world appeared to her holding this cross, now adorned with precious stones, in his hand. "Daughter," he said, "do you recognize this cross?" "I certainly do," replied Catherine, "but when it was mine it was not so beautiful." Said the Lord, "I promise you that I will present it to you, just as it is now, in the presence of the angels and men on Judgment Day."

Another day the Lord appeared to her in the likeness of a young man half-naked. She said to him, "Wait here for me a little while, while I go back into that chapel, and then I will give you clothing." Once inside the chapel, she carefully and modestly pulled down the sleeveless tunic that she wore under her outer tunic and gave it to the poor beggar. He no sooner accepted it than he made another request: "Lady, now that you have supplied me with a woolen garment, will you give me some linen clothes too?" Catherine said, "Follow me." Entering her home, she went into the room where the linen clothes belonging to her father and brothers were kept, took out a shirt and a pair of trousers and with a smile offered them to the beggar. But he said, "Lady, what use is this tunic to me without sleeves?" Whereupon Catherine, not in the least degree put out by this, set off on a careful search of the house. She happened to see the serving woman's dress hanging from a pole, so she quickly unstitched the sleeves, and gave them to the beggar.

He then said, "Look, lady, you have given me a new set of clothing, but I have a friend and he too is in great need of clothing." Catherine remembered that everyone in the house except her father was upset at her continual almsgiving. So she was in two minds as to what to do, whether to give the poor fellow her one remaining piece of clothing or not. Charity suggested she should, but maidenly modesty said no. So she said to the beggar, "If it was lawful for me to go about without a tunic I would give you this one gladly; but I am not allowed to do so." The other replied, "I know you would be very pleased to give me all you could. Farewell."

During the night, while she was praying, there appeared to her the Savior of the world, in the likeness of this beggar, holding in his hand the tunic that Catherine had given him, now decked out with pearls and brilliant gems; and He said to her, "Most beloved daughter, do you recognize this tunic?" When she answered that she did, but that she had not given it to Him in that rich state, the Lord went on, "Yesterday, you clothed me; now I will give you from my holy Body a piece of clothing that will certainly be invisible to the eyes of men but which you nevertheless will be able to perceive, and by means of it your soul and body will be protected against all danger of cold until the time comes for you to be clothed with glory and honor in the presence of the saints and angels." And immediately with His most holy hands He drew forth from the wound in His side a garment the color of blood, and putting it upon her, He said, "I give you this garment with all its powers for the rest of your life on earth, as a sign and token of the garment of glory with which at the appropriate time you will be clothed in heaven." With this the vision vanished.

The holy virgin from that time forward never wore any more clothes in winter than she did in summer.[11]

St. Vincent de Paul's charism of love for the poor and for all those in need continues to shine like a beacon down through the centuries. When he explained their Rule to the first Daughters of Charity, he went so far as to say:

You should know, my daughters, that when you set aside your prayers or the holy Mass in order to serve the poor you will not be losing anything, because serving the poor means going to visit God, and in the poor person you ought to see God.[12]

But let us now look at another great saint of the poor, who made himself poverty for love of Christ. We all know him: Francis of Assisi. He had such a deep sense of universal brotherhood, that he could not conceive of a world with social inequalities, in which some have more and some have less. It is certainly not by chance that he is referred to as the saint most similar to Christ.

One day while he was riding on horseback through the plain that lies below the town of Assisi, he came upon a leper. This unforeseen encounter struck him with horror. But he recalled his resolution...to become a knight of Christ. He...ran to kiss the man. When the leper put out his hand as if to receive some alms, Francis gave him money and a kiss. Immediately mounting his horse, Francis looked all around; but although the open plain stretched clear in all directions, he could not see the leper anywhere. Filled with wonder and joy, he began devoutly to sing God's praises....[13]

When he met [the poor] he not only generously gave them even the necessities of life that had been given to him, but he believed that these should be given them as if theirs by right. It happened once that a poor man met him...when because of an illness [Francis] was wearing a short mantle over his habit. When his kind eye observed the man's misery, he said to his companion: "We should return this mantle to this poor man because it is his. For we got it on loan until we should find someone poorer than ourselves." But his companion, considering the need of his devoted father, obstinately refused, lest Francis provide for another by neglecting himself. But Francis said: "I believe that the great Almsgiver will charge me with theft if I do not give what I have to one who needs it more." Therefore concerning all that was given him to relieve the needs of his body, he was accustomed to ask the permission of the donors to give it away if he should meet someone in greater need. He spared nothing at all, neither mantles, tunics nor books, not even decorations from the altar—

all these he gave to the poor when he could.... [14]

Jesus in those who suffer, according to Paul VI

Let us now see how Pope Paul VI looked upon those who suffer. His words to the convicts of Rome, when he visited them in 1965, are a sublime affirmation that he saw Jesus in them:

I love you; not because of some romantic feeling, not because of some compassionate humanitarian impulse, but I truly love you because even now I am discovering in you the image of God, the likeness of Christ....

And now I will tell you...a paradox...a truth which doesn't seem true.... The Lord Jesus... has taught us that it is your misfortune, your hurt, your lacerated and faulty humanity which constitutes the very reason for which I have come among you, to love you, to assist you, to console you, and to tell you that you are the image of Christ, that you reproduce the crucified Christ before my eyes.... This is why I have come...to fall on my knees before you.... [15]

On another occasion, speaking about those dedicated to caring for suffering children, he said:

They are destined to be in a sort of perpetual adoration, not of Jesus in his real presence under the Eucharistic species, but of what Bossuet called "the human presence of Jesus Christ in those who suffer."[16]

Paul VI himself explained the presence of Jesus in the poor and the suffering in this way:

We must remember that Jesus is the Son of Man: it was he who named and defined himself this way.... This means that every human being, every human life, has a connection with him. Jesus is involved in a relationship with every creature, and therefore he has a relationship with everyone who suffers.... Jesus draws to himself every human suffering; not only because he is the one who has suffered in the highest degree and as a result of the greatest injustice, but also because... he has immense affection and sympathy...for those who suffer.[17]

We have now considered some of the aspects of the presence of Jesus in those who suffer. May we never ever forget that we belong to the Church of the poor, and that the Movement must therefore be the Movement of the poor; all the more so, since this is nothing other than Christianity. At the end of our lives—as we have seen—our final examination will be on this very subject: the so-called "works of mercy." Pope John Paul I said: "The catechism translates this [passage about the Last Judgment in Mt. 25:31-46] into the two lists of the works of mercy, seven corporal and seven spiritual."[18]

So let us rectify our intentions, and thereby transform every act of love toward every neighbor in need—whether at home, at work, in school, on the street, or anywhere else—into one of the works of mercy. In this way we will open wide the doors of our hearts to all those we find out about each day who are miserable, abandoned, sick, sinners, alienated, rejected, the dregs of society, or whose human rights are trampled on, whether they are in our own cities and countries or in faraway places.

The poor and the Movement

Just as we find the poor around the new-born baby Jesus, just as taking care of the poor was one of the main concerns of the early Christian community, just as the saints have often begun their ascent to God by going out to the poor, similarly, around the first signs of life of our Movement we find the poor.

I was still living at home on Via Gocciadoro when the first Focolarine[19] and I began this new adventure. I do not know exactly what it was that impelled us to go out with such zeal to the poor of the city of Trent, and to continue this zealous activity later on in the first Focolare. I think it must have been the words of Jesus, "Whatever you did to the least you did to me" (see Mt. 25:40).

I remember the rather long corridor of my house filled with anything that could be of use to the poor: cases of jam, cans of powdered milk, sacks of flour, clothes, medicine, and firewood.

I remember that we had very little time, because all of us were working or going to school. So at lunch time, as soon as we had finished eating, we would set out for the three poorest neighborhoods in the city: Androne, Laste, and Portella. Each of us carried two packed and heavy suitcases. It was always a race!

It meant climbing dark flights of stairs, old and dangerous, eaten away by time and vermin, into almost total darkness, into desolate situations which pained our young hearts. Having mounted the stairs, we would find a room without light, its poor occupant in bed, generally lacking everything. It was Jesus. We would wash and console him, make promises in the name of Almighty God, and give whatever we could.

On one occasion, a Focolarina was loving Jesus in a

poor woman with all her heart. She remained in the woman's house for some time, giving it a thorough cleaning, and finally sang her a song dedicated to mothers. Afterward, she found she had caught an infection which produced open sores all over her face. But immediately she was happy because she was able to be a little bit similar to Jesus forsaken.

Whenever a poor person would come to our homes, we would choose the best tablecloth, the best dishes and tableware. Frequently what we gave him or her to eat consisted of what we had deprived ourselves of at lunch or dinner, by slipping our bread, cheese or whatever under the table when our parents were not looking, and involving our little sisters in the game as well.

When we went out each of us carried a pocket notebook, and our hearts would jump for joy whenever we met a poor person. We would approach him or her with great love and ask for his or her name and address so that we would be able to love "to the end."

Yes, for although our immediate concern was certainly to help each individual poor person, from the start we did so with a very precise plan in mind: we wanted to resolve the social problem of the city of Trent. God did not let us see anything else, almost as if, once it were accomplished, all the world's problems would have been solved. And so we focused our efforts on those who lived in the destitute areas of the city, in order to alleviate their condition: first, by providing them with medicine, food, and wood for heat; and, later on, by finding jobs for them.

Quite often episodes occurred in which it was evident that God had intervened to encourage us, and some of these are still recounted today.

In the first Focolare on Piazza Cappuccini the work continued just as intensely. Each day we would make a huge pot of soup which we would then take to the poor in a neighborhood called San Martino. But the poor people also regarded the Focolare as their home, and they would come and eat with us; and at table there would be a poor person, then a Focolarina, a poor person, a Focolarina, and so on.

Then the war ended, and the poor became better-off; and gradually we began to disperse throughout Italy to announce the Gospel we had rediscovered.

But wherever the Movement has since spread throughout the world, whenever there has been a need, as in Cameroun or Brazil, or parts of Asia; or whenever the Gen (the "New Generation" of the Focolare Movement) have repeated the experience of the first generation, whether the context was similar or not, the poor have always been with us.

Moreover, the Movement as a whole is now experiencing a new springtime as regards going out to assist others, through the Movement for a New

Humanity, which is animated by members of the Focolare Movement and guided by its spirit. This Movement for a New Humanity has timidly but decisively put itself at the service of society, particularly today's poor: the drug addicts, the alienated, the unemployed, the sinners, the amoral, the unbelievers.

"Die for our people" is the motto of this operation which re-echoes and relives what Jesus did.

In this way we live and work, awaiting the day when Jesus can say to all of us: "I was an outsider and you brought me into your community, I was on drugs and you gave me back true happiness, I was unemployed and you found me a job. I had no standards to live by, and you taught me God's law. I was without God, and you made me rediscover him as Love, by drawing me into your own divine adventure."

4

Christ and the non-Christians

Christians and the faithful of other religions

The Movement's experience

For some time now, due to its expansion throughout the world, the Movement has been coming into contact with many members of non-Christian faiths, even though it has only recently begun giving this immense number of believers (1.5 billion in 1965) very special consideration.

Our attitude toward these non-Christian brothers and sisters has been to love them. And love itself has been a source of light, enabling us to know how to approach them.

Love, which induces Christians to be the first to love, prompted us to take an interest in everything that concerns them: from their worries about their families, work, school, and social condition, to their spiritual concerns and so on, all the way up to their religious beliefs.

Christian love may seem like mere human friendship, but if it is prompted by supernatural motives it causes us not only to give to others but to confide in them, to give what we have and what we are. And so, these brothers and sisters of ours have come to know everything about us, from the little things to our great ideal: Christ, who has taken first place in our lives.

This was possible, still is, and always will be, because with love as our starting point, we have found glimmers of Gospel truth in their religious thought. And in their lives we have found acts full of sacrifice and love for others, along with principles which are sound and universally acceptable. On this basis we are able to make a serene and peaceful comparison between their faith and ours, between their life and the Christian life.

This results in an indirect evangelization of these brothers and sisters, who accept dialogue based on love and life, and subsequently also accept dialogue on matters of faith. At the same time it provokes a common desire to take seriously those elements which already unite us and to live them, in order to work together to make the world better through religion. As a result, they are not reluctant to unite themselves to our Movement, participating in our meetings and in the life of the Movement's various branches, as Muslim or Buddhist Gen or Volunteers, Buddhist or Hindu monks or nuns, and so on.

This has been our small experience, which is still continuing and which we hope will take on ever larger dimensions in the future.

Vatican II and the non-Christian religions[1]

Let us now look at what the Church—and in particular Vatican II—teaches about the faithful of other religions and about the relationships that Christians should have with them. We will avail ourselves of the Council documents so that our own work may have a broader approach, greater depth, and a stronger foundation.

The Council acknowledged that "the Holy Spirit was already at work in the world before Christ was glorified,"[2] and believed that the same Holy Spirit is also at work today among non-Christians. Therefore, "the Catholic Church rejects nothing which is true and holy in these religions."[3]

The Council recognized that numerous elements of truth and grace are to be found among the non-Christians, as a sort of hidden presence of God,[4] and acknowledged that their religions "often reflect a ray of that truth which enlightens all men."[5] Moreover, it speaks of "the seeds of the Word which lie hidden in them [the non-Christians]."[6]

Justin, a second-century philosopher and martyr, held that the divine Word (Logos) is wholly present only in Jesus, but that, given the instrumental role of the Word in creation, "seeds of the Word"[7] have been sown throughout the whole of humanity, so that in every human being there is a seed of the Word.

73

The *Decree on the Church's Missionary Activity* also recognizes "the ascetic and contemplative traditions whose seeds were sometimes already planted by God in ancient cultures prior to the preaching of the gospel."[8] Moreover, it says that all these spiritual and religious values, which are found both in the individual non-Christians and in their rites and cultures, "through the kindly workings of Divine Providence, may sometimes serve as a guidance course toward the true God, or as a preparation for the gospel."[9]

However, since "rather often men, deceived by the Evil One, have become caught up in futile reasoning and have exchanged the truth of God for a lie, serving the creature rather than the Creator,"[10] they need the Church's presence. For "[the Church's missionary] activity frees from all taint of evil and restores to Christ its maker whatever truth and grace are to be found among the nations."[11]

This means that the behavior of individual Christians as well, must be characterized by prudence and discernment.[12]

How Christians should act toward members of other religions[13]

Vatican II lays great stress on how Christians should behave toward non-Christians. It encourages them to "gladly and reverently" uncover "the seeds of the Word which lie hidden in them [the non-Christians]." And it goes on to say:

> ...Christians should know the people among whom they live, and should establish contact with them. Thus they themselves can learn by sincere and patient dialogue what treasures a bountiful God has distributed among the nations of the earth. But at the same time, let them try to illumine these treasures with the light of the gospel....[14]

The Council also urges that the exposition of the Word of God be adapted to the customs, culture, and mentality of the various peoples, and that "theological investigation" be fostered, avoiding, of course, "every appearance of syncretism and of false particularism."[15]

> Anything in their way of life that is not indissolubly bound up with superstition and error she [the Church] studies with sympathy and, if possible, preserves intact. Sometimes in fact she admits such things into the liturgy itself....[16]

And finally, the Council invites all Christians to work together with non-Christians for peace, justice, freedom, and religion.[17] And in the *Dogmatic*

Constitution on the Church, it makes the following very clear affirmation:

> ...those who have not yet received the gospel are related in various ways to the People of God. In the first place there is the people to whom the Covenants and the promises were given and from whom Christ was born according to the flesh....
>
> But the plan of salvation also includes those who acknowledge the Creator. In the first place among these are the Muslims.... Nor is God Himself far distant from those who in shadows and images seek the unknown God, for it is He who gives to all men life...and who as Savior wills that all men be saved (see 1 Tim. 2:4).[18]

The human person as viewed by the great religions

Let us now—though in a necessarily limited way—consider some of the more important non-Christian religions, and see what importance they give to one's neighbor—or better, to human beings as such.

The Judaic tradition

I will not pause now to further consider the Judaic

view of the human person, since we have already taken a look at what the Old Testament has to say on the subject, and we have seen that love of neighbor is one of its central norms.

It is unnecessary to say that for us Christians, the Jews are our closest brothers and sisters, because of the immense divine truths which we have in common and which bind us together. It is logical to think that one of these days Jesus will illuminate these blood relatives of his with the full light of the truth, because it is impossible for him not to love them in a very special way, after all the extra-ordinary graces that God has poured out on them as his chosen people.

The Islamic tradition

Let us move on to Islam.

Faith in Islam is witness: "There is no God but Allah ["the God"]; and Muhammad is the Messenger of Allah." This is the formula for the profession of faith which incorporates one into Islam and makes one a "believer" and, after death, a "guest of paradise."

This faith is a gift of God. It demands first of all the witness and the adherence of the heart, which renders one "a believer in the eyes of God." It also demands a spoken witness, which makes one "a believer in the eyes of men." And finally it demands that witness be given by carrying out the works prescribed by the Law.

The precepts of the divine Law are found in the Koran (which contains God's revelations to Muhammad). They govern religious practices and lay down norms for all human activity. The principal religious observances prescribed are known traditionally as "the Pillars of Islam" and are: the proclamation of the profession of faith (given above); ritual prayer to be performed five times a day; almsgiving according to the Law; fasting during the month of Ramadan; pilgrimage to Mecca at least once during one's lifetime. There are numerous other precepts which include instructions regarding food, funerals, visits to cemeteries, marriage and family life, and relationships in society.

Even though the witness of faith saves one directly ("those whose heart contains an atom of faith will escape hell"), in large areas of the Muslim world today it seems that faith without works, without some moral and civil commitment, is less and less acceptable. For a sincere Muslim today, "good works" are often more important than an external observance of the Pillars of Islam. Moreover, many passages in the Koran stress the duty to help one's neighbor; to come to the assistance of orphans, the poor, the unhappy; to keep one's word; to welcome travelers; to ransom prisoners; and so on.[19]

In Islam as well, therefore, one's neighbor is given some consideration.

Muslim customs, which are based on the *aklaq,* are also strict. And in the Koran, frequent passages on how to behave toward one's neighbor call to mind the content of the commandments in Exodus and Deuteronomy.

> You shall show kindness to your parents; you shall not kill your children because you cannot support them (We provide for you and for them); you shall not commit foul sins, whether openly or in secret; and you shall not kill—for that is forbidden by Allah—except for a just cause (Koran 6:151).
>
> Allah enjoins justice, kindness and charity to one's kindred (Koran 16:90).[20]

Moreover, the Koran condemns adultery, fornication, homosexuality, stealing, and giving false testimony.

Muslim morality, therefore, is based on God. But in spite of the value given to "works," good or bad actions which do not directly involve faith still have only relative importance when compared to giving witness to the one God and to his Messenger.[21]

Islam is a religion, but it is also inseparably community, culture, and civilization. However, it is not a "state" in the modern juridical sense of the

79

term. The "community of believers" may coincide with a single empire, as it did in earlier times, or with a multitude of sultanates, kingdoms, and republics, as it does today.

As a member of the "community of the Prophet," the Muslim feels that he is a "believer" and that he is "entrusted to God." And in the community he finds strength, peace, and the full development of his human dignity.[22]

Among the strongest sociological realities of the Muslim world is brotherhood. The Koran says: "Remember the favours He has bestowed upon you: how He united your hearts when you were enemies, so that you are now brothers through His grace" (Koran 3:103).

However, this brotherhood is only open to those who wish to embrace Islam, and equality among all men takes effect only after their conversion. Even so, Islam's attitude toward the "People of the Book" (Jews and Christians) is different from its attitude toward pagans.

For although the Koran recognizes the obligation to show hospitality and to give to those in need, it is severe toward pagans, who are considered enemies: "Muhammad is Allah's apostle. Those who follow him are ruthless to the unbelievers [polytheists] but merciful to one another" (Koran 48:29).

In Islam one does not go to God by means of loving one's neighbor, nor is God to be found in our fellow human beings, nor does faith lose any of its value if there is no fraternal love. Kindness toward one's neighbor—or, better, toward one's fellow Muslim—can, at most, bring one to faith in God, but in just the same way as would any of the other "good works" or religious practices. Such benevolent love, by virtue of the fact that it unites people, is a preparation for the revelation of the unity of God.[23]

For this reason, those Focolarine and Focolarini who have been in contact with Muslims affirm that the way to present our religion to these brothers and sisters is to live in perfect unity among ourselves, in a unity that is stronger than theirs because of the presence of Christ in our midst (see Mt. 18:20).

Our belief in the Trinity of God arouses reservations and misunderstandings among Muslims because they fear that it is against the unity of God. But this strong unity among us, since it gives witness to the unity of God, makes them think of the one and only God who is at the heart of their faith, and in whom we also believe.

Hindu perspectives

Hinduism is the result of the history of a people who has dedicated its finest energies to the pursuit of the spiritual. The fixed point in this quest, the milestone to which reference is always made is the intuition that Reality is One.

81

The gods, humans, the world, all the things that have been, are, or ever will be: all this is one and the same Reality: "The whole universe is Brahman" (*Chāndogya Upanishad* III, 14, 1). And when a person has reached the state of enlightenment, he or she may also say: "I am Brahman" (*Brihadāranyaka Upanishad* I, 4, 10). Brahman is "one only—without a second" (*Chāndogya Upanishad* VI, 2, 1-3).

The innermost self—Atman—of a person is also identical with Brahman: "He is my Self within the heart, smaller than a grain of rice or a barley corn, or a mustard seed, or a grain of millet; this is my Self within my heart, greater than the earth, greater than the atmosphere, greater than the sky.... This my Self within the heart is that Brahman" (Ibid. III, 14, 3-4). And as far as the individual is concerned, for centuries Hinduism has been repeating the phrase of Uddalaka to his son Svetaketu: "That [Brahman-Atman] *you* are!" (Ibid. VI 8,7; 9,4; 10,3; 11,3; 12,3; 13,3; 14,3; 15,3; 16,2).

In this way the Brahman-Atman is recognized as the sole Absolute, the root and foundation of everything, the Lord who upholds and sustains all things, the inner guide and the goal of every living thing....

Everything that is apparent is the selfsame Brahman who manifests himself through each thing. He is the true Reality of every one of his manifestations. Only if a phenomenon is considered on its own can we speak of beginning or end, of birth or death; but the phenomenon itself has always been in the bosom of Brahman, and will be conserved in Him eternally.

Not only does one not die, but in reality one has never been born: "Never was there a time when I was not, nor you, nor yet these lords of men; nor will there be a time when we shall cease to be—all of us hereafter. Just as in this body the embodied soul must pass through childhood, youth and age, so too at death will he take another body up" (*Bhagavad-Gita* II, 12-13)....

[Therefore] the deepest Self of every human being, his true Person, is the Atman and that is identical to Brahman: "indestructible, eternal, unborn, never to pass away.... As a man casts off his worn-out clothes and takes on other new ones, so does the embodied soul cast off his worn-out bodies and enters others new" (Ibid. II, 20-25).[24]

Therefore, in the words of P. Rossano:

83

In the monistic view of Hinduism, earthly reality actually disappears: "It is not for the love of a husband that a husband is dearly loved. Rather it is for love of the Self [Atman] that a husband is dearly loved.... It is not for the love of a wife that a wife is dearly loved. Rather it is for love of the Self [Atman] that a wife is dearly loved.... It is not for love of [anything] that [anything] is dearly loved. Rather it is for love of the Self [Atman] that [anything] is dearly loved" (*Brihadāranyaka Upanishad* II, 4, 5). Nothing is loved for its own sake, but always for love of Atman. The Atman is all that is.[25]

One can understand, then, the words of another author:

Love of the neighbor as such is scarcely ever directly enjoined in the Hindu Scriptures, and one would search in vain for anything like the "new commandment" of the Gospel.... According to the *Īśā Upanishad,* he who sees all things in the Self (Atman) and the Self in all things, does not shrink back or run away from anything. It is impossible for him to esteem more highly the "manifestation" of the Atman, the unique Self, in his own body and mind than the "manifestation" of the same unique Self in the body and mind of anyone else. In the light of that Self he cannot experience, or even think of, himself as separate from others. His awareness of himself as a particular thinking and perceiving individual is completely shot through with the awareness of the Self as unparticularized and unconditioned. He truly loves "himself" in every being.[26]

And is thus liberated from all egoism.

But whatever might be the practical consequences of this formulation of Hindu wisdom [such as frequent indifference toward the physical and spiritual needs of one's neighbor], the real *jnani* [wise man] loves uniquely well, and all who have met such a *jnani* will testify to this fact. No matter what philosophy he employs to express his outlook, the *jnani's* actions, the look in his eyes, and his consideration for each individual, all speak eloquently of the love that fills his heart. He is entirely transparent to the Spirit, and there is nothing in him to obstruct the moving of the Spirit; from his heart the Spirit flows forth to every heart. . . . He is all things to all men, to every man. For himself he demands and expects nothing, since all that comes to him passes through him to the Lord himself within him.[27]

God is living in these non-Christian contemplatives and manifesting himself—unknown to them—for what he is: Love.

Toward the third century B.C., alongside the absolute monism of Hinduism, a new and flourishing doctrine appeared: Bhakti, centered on God's love for Man and Man's love for God.[28] Whereas Brahman is impersonal, in Bhakti God is also personal. Moreover, the external world and individual souls are not lost in the divinity, but seem to possess a consistency of their own. In Bhakti, which means "devotion," "love," Man is engaged in a "loving, trusting flight toward God."[29]

All this must stimulate us Christians to live up to the Gospel with all its demands—since it is the revelation of God who is Love—so that there will not be just a few saints who give witness to God, but a great part of Christendom will give witness to him.

Then many of those young people who in their search for the spiritual are investigating the ways of India will find among the followers of Christ the ideal they are looking for.

Buddhist perspectives

Buddhism was initially a purely ethical doctrine, which through the centuries has developed into various religious sects and philosophical schools.

The intention of Buddha ("the Enlightened One"), after his personal experience, was only to show others the way to reach freedom from suffering and from endless reincarnation. Reincarnation—inherited from Hinduism—is considered an undisputed truth in Buddhism.

For Buddha, everything in the world is suffering and sorrow, because everything is transitory. Man himself is also composed of psycho-physical elements which are continually changing with no permanent or unchanging principle—therefore with no soul.

Buddha taught that the source of suffering is desire, whatever form this desire may take, because everything that one desires to have or to be is only transitory.

In order to extinguish suffering, therefore, one must suppress all desires, eradicate passions and selfishness, subdue every affirmation of one's ego. In this way—while still in this life, and even more so after one's physical death—through one's own efforts one may reach "Nirvana," the state of complete freedom from all desire, of the absolute absence of suffering, of indescribable peace, in which the painful cycle of reincarnation is broken.

One can only reach this state gradually through the practice of the Eightfold Path of the Buddhist ethic. Detachment from everything is a requirement for everyone. However, this is only carried out completely in the monastic life, in which one "seeks refuge" not only "in Buddha" and "in the Law," but also "in the community" as such.[30] For in the community, one finds the best conditions for reaching that full illumination which allows one to intuit the true nature of things—which is their "emptiness"—and in this way to extinguish all desire.

Regarding relationship with one's neighbor, Buddhism stresses the practice of virtue, particularly benevolence and unselfish love, in order to purify the heart of attachments. But it does not consider love as the way to human perfection nor as an integral part of it.

Through the centuries, Buddhism has split into two main currents or schools. Mahayana (the "greater vehicle"), more open to the people, has introduced a greater concern for others into the earlier doctrine of Theravada Buddhism (the "way of the elders").

The innovations of Mahayana Buddhism derive from a new definition of the Buddha and a new conception of Man. Buddha is "Nothingness," "Emptiness,"—not an emptiness of being, but the absence of every dialectic and of every human category. He transcends them. He is the Absolute itself (*solutus ab:* "freed from"). He is infinite light, infinite life, infinite mercy. "The Buddha is love"

(*Kan-mu-ryo-ju-kyo*), "he is the infinite love which pardons all" (*Mahaprajnaparamita-sutra*, 27). He is "the Father and the Savior of all creatures" (*Saddharmapundarika-sutra*, 18). And "every person potentially possesses the nature of Buddha" (*Mahaparinirvana-sutra*, 27). Therefore, to the Mahayana Buddhist, denying oneself is the indispensable condition for activating this potential, for allowing Buddha to live in him.[31]

From the new vision of Buddha and of human nature comes also the need to love one's neighbor....

The apex of Mahayana asceticism consists of seeing Buddha in everyone and everyone in Buddha....

Particularly significant in this regard is the following allegory: "Imagine a thousand watery surfaces: that of a large river or of a large lake, of a clear fountain or of a dirty puddle. All of them reflect the moon. The moon reflected on one of these thousand surfaces is not the thousandth part of the moon, but the one and entire moon. One sees a thousand moons, but in reality there is only one moon in the sky. As there are a thousand reflections of the same moon, so men are many reflections of the same Buddha: small or great, miserable or holy—this does not matter. The moon reflected is always the whole moon. Buddha also is always entire in men" (Inscription of Hsin-hsin-ming).

According to Mahayana doctrine, every person is a *bodhisattva;* that is, a being destined for enlightenment. In order to reach this enlightenment he takes a vow to become Buddha, he asks his help and commits himself to the serious practice of these virtues: "generosity toward all, morality in living, patience even toward enemies, vigor, contemplation, and wisdom."

All the actions of the *bodhisattva* must be motivated by love toward all creatures.... "To serve creatures is to serve Buddha, is to fulfill my purpose, is to eliminate the world's suffering" (*Bodhicaryavatara,* VI, 127).

The *bodhisattva*...works untiringly for the salvation of all creatures, without ever desiring to enter Nirvana until he has saved all the others: "The compassionate man [the *bodhisattva*], who with the strength of wisdom has uprooted all self-love, because of his love for all creatures never withdraws into Peace [Nirvana]" (*Ratnagotra-vibha-sastra,* 35).

...Therefore the Mahayana Buddhist wishes to remain in the world of reincarnation for the total Buddhafication of the universe. This is Mahayanan salvation: "Whoever does not save the others does not save even himself" (*Mu-chu-mon-do-shu,* 49).[32]

In short, the older Theravada Buddhism seeks self-liberation from suffering and relies only on human efforts. Mahayana Buddhism, on the other hand, teaches trust in the help that can come from above and a great openness toward others.

Christ and nonbelievers

We have taken a rapid look at what sort of consideration the major religions give to Man.

Now let us see what relationship exists between Christ and members of non-Christian religions as well as nonbelievers.

Jesus said that his earthly mission concerned Israel (see Mt. 15:24), but his thinking and his behavior were stupendously open. He offered a Samaritan to the Jews as a model. He stated that "he that is not against us is for us" (Mk. 9:40), even if the person is not one of his disciples. He admired the faith of the centurion and of the Canaanite woman: they are signs and preludes of the fact that "men will come from east and west, and from north and south, and sit at table in the kingdom of God" (Lk. 13:29). He asks for love of enemies, and he

91

cares for the sinner and those who suffer, no matter who they are.

We must also take another look at the scene of the Last Judgment (Mt. 25:31-46), included in the preceeding chapter, especially Jesus' words: "As you did it to one of the least of these my brethren, you did it to me." According to the majority of Scripture scholars, the phrase "the least of these my brethren" refers to anyone in need, whether Christian or non-Christian. In fact, the context in which Jesus says these words is universal. He has before him "all the nations"—that is, all peoples, without restriction (see also Mt. 28:19).

In this text the evangelist's intention is certainly not to describe in detail how the Final Judgment will be carried out, but to tell us that love is the criterion on which everyone will be judged. In fact, each person who performs concrete acts of love will receive the kingdom as an inheritance: he or she will be saved. Therefore, every person who loves, whether aware of it or not, enters into direct contact with Christ, into a relationship with him, and is his brother or sister.

Therefore, every person who loves is acting under the influence of grace. As the Council states:

> Since Christ died for all men, and since the ultimate vocation of man is in fact one, and

divine, we ought to believe that the Holy Spirit in a manner known only to God offers to every man the possibility of being associated with this paschal mystery.[33]

Salvation, therefore, is for "all men of good will," that is for those who respond to the secret call of their hearts, in which "grace works in an unseen way."[34]

The ways by which non-Christians and non-believers are saved[35]

The Council brings out the fact that non-Christians, even nonbelievers, can come to the knowledge of God and attain salvation through created things and through following their own conscience.

The *Dogmatic Constitution on Divine Revelation* states that "God, who through the Word creates all things and keeps them in existence, gives men an enduring witness to Himself in created realities."[36]

And the *Pastoral Constitution on the Church in the Modern World* declares:

Conscience is the most secret core and sanctuary of a man. There he is alone with God, whose voice echoes in his depths. In a wonderful manner

93

conscience reveals that law which is fulfilled by love of God and neighbor (see Mt. 22:37-40; Gal. 5:14).[37]

There is no doubt that the Council considers that love for God, even if he is imperfectly known, and love for neighbor, when it is demonstrated by actions, are useful ways that "help men to attain to salvation."[38]

Moreover, the Council sees the Spirit of God at work in the progress of the social order which aims at promoting the welfare of the human person.[39] And it also sees his active presence in the area of scientific research: "Indeed, whoever labors to penetrate the secrets of reality with a humble and steady mind, is, even unaware, being led by the hand of God. . . ."[40]

Furthermore, the *Dogmatic Constitution on the Church* says:

Nor does divine Providence deny the help necessary for salvation to those who, without blame on their part, have not yet arrived at an explicit knowledge of God, but who strive to live a good life, thanks to His grace. Whatever goodness or truth is found among them is looked upon by the Church as a preparation for the gospel.[41]

94

Christians and non-Christians

In his Gospel, John affirms: "He who does what is true comes to the light, that it may be clearly seen that his deeds have been wrought in God" (2:31). Therefore, the person "who does what is true" (that is, what is good) is already "in God," in a certain communion with him. And this is clear.

To be "in God," however, is the foundation; it is not yet full communion with him. This full communion comes about only in the encounter with Christ. In a recent ecumenical translation of the Bible we find this comment: "The one who does what is good is already in a certain communion with God and is tending toward the full encounter which takes place in his Son."[42]

The Father brings all those who belong to him to Christ (see Jn. 17:6). Indeed, he is at work deep within each person's life—while fully respecting his or her freedom—preparing each one to meet Jesus: "no one can come to me unless the Father who sent me draws him.... Everyone who has heard and learned from the Father comes to me" (Jn. 6:44-45).

The full encounter with Jesus demands a new birth, which only the Spirit can bring about (as we have seen in speaking of the presence of Jesus in the Christian). Then, according to Paul, the person becomes a "new creation" in Christ (2 Cor. 5:17).

He or she is renewed in the depths of his or her being (see 2 Cor. 4:16). The acceptance of the Gospel—the encounter with Jesus—transforms a person. It truly makes of him or her a new being; it unites him or her ontologically and vitally to the risen Christ. This is what constitutes the "newness of life" (Rom. 6:4) in which the Christian lives.

The task of the Church

At times non-Christians are referred to as being "Christians implicitly," or as "anonymous Christians," or as "Christians who don't know they are Christians." But this does not mean that the only difference between them and Christians lies in knowing or not knowing that one is a Christian. Nor is the work of the Church merely aimed at rendering explicit a reality which persons of good will might already possess.

The Council states that Christ, through his Spirit, "had established His body, the Church, as the universal sacrament of salvation.... He is continually active in the world, leading men to the Church, and through her joining them more closely to Himself...."[43] And in himself, he unites them to the Father and to one another.

This explains the active role of the Church and,

above all, its task to "preach the gospel to the whole creation" (Mk. 16:15).

Every person on earth, if he or she is "of good will," is a candidate for heaven. This means that even as it strives toward the day "that they may all be one" (Jn. 17:21), the Church already embraces, in one way or another, all the good that exists in the world.

5

How to love our neighbor

The path to reach God

God gives each one who seeks him a way to find him. And often each person is convinced that his or her way is the shortest route to reach him.

I suppose no one could have made St. Theresa of Avila doubt that she had discovered the fastest way to get to God. She says that if you want to find God, you had better look for him where he is: in the center of your heart.

St. Francis finds God through nature as well. His "Canticle of the Sun," which is intended to embrace the whole universe, reveals his concept of God: he is Creator and Father of all that exists. Therefore, animals and flowers, the sun, the moon and the stars, and men and women are all brothers and sisters.

It would be beautiful if we could get to know one by one the ways that God has opened up for people to reach him; this is what the followers of the various saints have always tried to do.

But let us consider our own case. Those familiar with the Movement know that when God called me to consecrate myself to him forever, the fascination of that call and the elation which flooded my whole being because I had married God were so unique and exceptional that I would have never ever wanted anyone or anything to break the enchantment of that one-to-one relationship with him. If they had told me that day that I was going to have companions, if they had revealed to me that a Movement was going to be born, I feel that something divine and inexpressible would have been broken.

But God very quickly made it clear to me, as only he knows how, that loving him involved doing something specific: loving him in my brothers and sisters, in every brother and sister in the world.

God's conception of human nature is something unimaginable! In 1949, I wrote:

> The Father, Jesus, Mary, us. The Father permitted Jesus to feel forsaken by him *for us*. Jesus accepted being forsaken by the Father and he deprived himself of his Mother *for us*. Mary shared Jesus' abandonment and accepted the loss of her Son *for us*. Therefore *we* are put in first place. It is love which does such crazy things. So we too, when God's will requires it, must leave the Father, Jesus, and Mary for our brother or sister.

Thus our neighbor took a definite place in our heart.

But "the one who loses finds" (see Mt. 10:39), and immediately it became clear to us that our neighbor was not to be loved merely for his or her own sake, but rather we had to love Christ in him or her. Jesus had said: "as you did it to one of the least of these my brethren [which includes everyone], you did it to me" (Mt. 25:40). Consequently, our whole previous way of looking at people and of loving them collapsed. If in some way Christ was in everyone, we could not practice discrimination or have preferences. Out went all the human criteria by which persons are classified as countryman or alien, old or young, beautiful or ugly, pleasant or unpleasant, rich or poor. Christ was behind each person; Christ was in each person. Every neighbor was truly another Christ if his or her soul was enriched with God's grace; and even if someone was without grace, he or she was still potentially another Christ.

Living in this manner we came to the realization that our neighbor was our way to God. Each brother or sister appeared to us as a doorway through which we had to pass in order to encounter God.

We experienced this right from the very first days. After having loved God all day in our brothers and sisters, in the evening, in recollection or in prayer, we would experience a wonderful union with him. Who could have given us that consolation, that inner peace, so new and heavenly, if not Christ who was living the words of his Gospel: "Give, and it will be given to you" (Lk. 6:38)? We had loved him all day in our neighbors, and now he was loving us.

These interior gifts were of great benefit to us. They were our first experiences of the spiritual life, of the reality of a kingdom which is not of this world. And so the Movement was able to begin its march through the world which does not belong to Christ, because our hearts had experienced that love which is not of the world.

The bond between love of God and love of neighbor

Our experience, therefore, tells us this: love of neighbor comes from love of God; but love for God blossoms in our hearts because we love our neighbor.

It was a comfort for me to find this same experience in Catherine of Siena. In her *Dialogue* she writes that the Eternal Father instructed her with these words:

Now I want to speak to you about the second mistake made by those who find all their delight in seeking spiritual consolation.... If these people are unable to have their consolations, they think they are committing sin; and instead... they do not see that they offend me more by not meeting the needs of their neighbor....

Since they do not help their neighbor, fraternal love diminishes in them; and when this love diminishes, so does my affection toward them. And when my affection for them diminishes, the consolations diminish as well."[1]

We have known from the very beginning of the Movement that there was a bond between love of God and love of neighbor. Igino Giordani[2] used to explain our way with this threefold expression: I— my neighbor—God.

Gregory the Great speaks masterfully about the relationship between love of God and love of neighbor, using an example which is also very familiar to us: the root and the plant.

There are two precepts regarding Charity: love of God and love of neighbor. Love of neighbor is born of love of God, and love of God is nourished by love of neighbor. For whoever neglects to love God, is quite incapable of love of neighbor. And we can advance more perfectly in love of God, if first, in the bosom of his love, we are nursed with the milk of love of neighbor. Since love of God generates love of neighbor, in giving the Law, the Lord first set down, "You shall love the Lord your God" (Dt. 6:5), before he said, "You shall love your neighbor" (Mt. 22:39). Thus, in the soil of our hearts he first planted the root of love toward him, and then, like foliage, fraternal love developed. And that the love of God is bound to love of neighbor is also attested to by John, when he says: "He who does not love his brother whom he has seen, cannot love God whom he has not seen" (1 Jn. 4:20).[3]

Isidore of Seville emphasized that "Charity consists in love of God and neighbor.... Whoever separates himself from fraternal communion is deprived of a share in God's love."[4] And the Curé of Ars warned: "Never lose sight of the fact that all the time you are not loving your neighbor, the good God is furious with you...."[5]

St. John of the Cross makes the following affirmation:

When one's love for a creature is purely spiritual and founded in God alone, then in the measure that it grows, love for God grows in one's soul as well. Then, the more the heart is aware of the neighbor, the more it is also aware of

God and desires him, the two loves vying to outdo each other as they grow.[6]

Thérèse of Lisieux copied the above words on the back of a holy picture for a novice who feared that she loved her novice mistress too much.

Edouard Dhanis beautifully portrays the love of neighbor as an "overflowing" of one's love for God onto one's fellow human beings. Our Movement thinks the same way.

> If one asks what is the way in which Jesus envisions the close union between fraternal love and love for God, we must answer that he views the first as an overflowing of the second. He wanted his disciples to put their hearts in unison with the heart of the heavenly Father—if I may use this expression—so that their love for God would extend to all those whom he loves as his children.... St. John indicated this with the following expression, rich in meaning: "Every one who loves the parent [God] loves the child [one's fellow human being]."...

And he goes on to say:

> One of the deeply comforting features in the countenance of the Church today—in the midst of

the crisis which is shaking her...is a sort of renewed understanding in many of the faithful of the primacy owed to the love of God and neighbor in the Christian life. This renewal is apparent in exegesis, and in moral and spiritual theology. I am referring to a reality that is intensely lived in some religious institutes and movements in which there is a full awareness that authentic Christian love cannot be lived without the cross of Jesus, but where—for this very reason—there reigns a joy which makes one think of heaven.[7]

The author notes that in so writing he had in mind the Little Brothers of Foucauld and the Focolare.

In an editorial in *La Civiltà Cattolica,* among other things, the writer tries to shed light on both the distinction and the bond between the two commandments: love God and love your neighbor. Love for God and love for one's neighbor, we are told, "were known to Jesus' contemporaries, because they are found in the Old Testament (Dt. 6:5; Lv. 19:18)."

What is characteristic about Jesus is the great emphasis he gives to these two commandments over all the others, and the bond he puts between them, making them into one double-faceted commandment and placing the foundation for love of neighbor in one's love for God.

Jesus gives pre-eminence to love for God.... He must be loved with absolute totality; that is, "with all your heart, with all your soul, and with all your mind" (Mt. 22:37)....

Jesus' love for his fellow human beings and his willingness to sacrifice himself for them spring from his love for the Father. In fact, as he is about to face his passion and death he says: "But the world must know that I love the Father and do as the Father has commanded me. Come then, let us go" (Jn. 14:31).[8]

It is Christ in us who must love our neighbor

To love our neighbor, every neighbor, as the Holy Spirit taught us to do at the beginning of the Movement, was an authentic revolution. At that time, the Christians whom we knew who were seeking the way to perfection tended to view their neighbor as an obstacle to their reaching God. They based their approach on spiritualities which were good, excellent, but which were primarily suited to those who were called to abandon the world and live in a monastery or convent. And so, at times, they deformed these spiritualities.

How could we have fled from other people, when we were called to live among them? The Lord used a special technique to teach us to love our neighbor, remaining in the world without being of the world. He immediately made us understand that it was possible for us to love our neighbor without falling into sentimentalism or other errors, because he himself could love in us, with his love: Charity. We were loving Christ in the other person, but it was also Christ in us who had to love.

And what is Charity? As we know, it is a love which comes from above. Paul says: "God's love has been poured into our hearts through the Holy Spirit which has been given to us" (Rom. 5:5). Charity, therefore, is a sharing in the divine *agape* (love). This Charity, this love, is spontaneous, always new; it continually finds different ways to express itself. It does not allow itself to be categorized. It invents unforeseeable solutions. Consequently, Paul tells us: "Be guided by the Spirit" (Gal. 5:16).

Charity is further characterized by unselfishness, initiative, universality, and the gift of oneself to the point of sacrifice.

In loving, a Christian must do as God does: not wait to be loved, but be the first to love. And since he or she cannot do this with God because he is always the first to love, the Christian puts this into practice with each neighbor. St. John tells us that God loves us, but he does not then conclude—as would have been more logical—that if God has loved us, we ought to love him in return. Instead he says: "Beloved, if God so loved us, we also ought to love one another" (1 Jn. 4:11).

It is only because Charity is a participation in God's love (*agape*), that we are able to go beyond natural limits to love our enemies and give our lives for our fellow human beings.

For this reason Christian love rightly belongs to the new era, and the "New" Commandment is radically new, and introduces something absolutely new into human history and human ethics. "This love," writes Augustine, "makes us new, so that we are new persons, heirs of the New Covenant, singers of the new song."[9]

If Charity is God's love shared with us, it is quite different from philanthropy. In fact, Christian love does not look at people from the point of view of their nature, but from the point of view of God's love for them, because it sees each person as a child of God, as his image.[10]

Likewise, Charity is not mere benevolence. As Leo the Great says: "Earthly benevolence reaches no further than the one it helps. But Christian goodness passes on to its Maker," that is, God himself. Therefore, when we do good, we can "be said to be doing good to him who we believe is at work within us."[11]

How Charity manifests itself

These lines from the Curé of Ars explain very well how Charity manifests itself. They seem to echo Paul's hymn to Charity.

"But," you will say, "how can we know that we have this beautiful and precious virtue, without which our religion is only an illusion?"

First of all, a person who possesses Charity is not proud; does not love to dominate others; can never be heard finding fault with others' conduct; does not love to speak about what others are doing. A person who has Charity does not question others' intentions;...does not believe he or she can do better than they; does not place himself or herself above his or her neighbor. On the contrary, such a person believes that others always do better, and does not take offence when a neighbor is preferred over him or her. When despised, one who possesses Charity remains happy nonetheless, thinking that he or she is deserving of even more contempt.

The person who has Charity avoids causing pain to others as much as possible, because Charity is a royal mantle which knows well how to hide the mistakes of one's brothers and sisters and never allows itself to think it is better than they are."[12]

112

According to Vincent de Paul, Charity can be expressed by our "making ourselves one" with our neighbor, which has been a characteristic of the Movement from its earliest years. "To make ourselves one" means to empty ourselves of ourselves in order to understand our neighbor and to put ourselves in his or her situation.

Charity is not being able to see a person suffer without suffering with him or her; or to see someone crying without crying with him or her. It is an act of love which causes hearts to penetrate one another and to feel what the other feels. It is very different from the actions of those people who do not feel anything when they see the torment of the afflicted and the suffering of the poor.

The Son of God had a tender heart. They came to call him to see Lazarus and he went. Mary Magdalen got up and ran out weeping to meet him. The Jews followed her, weeping as well. Everyone was weeping. What did the Lord do? He had so much tenderness and compassion in his soul that he wept with them. It was this tenderness of his which caused him to come down from heaven: he saw the human race deprived of his own glory; he was touched by their misfortune. So we too, like him, must be moved by the sufferings of our neighbor and share his or her sorrow. Oh Saint Paul, how sensitive you were to these sufferings! Oh Savior, who filled this apostle with your Spirit and your tenderness, grant that we also may be able to repeat with him: "Who can be sick, and I not sick with him?"

To be Christians and to see our own brother or sister suffering, and not suffer with him or her, not be sick with him or her, means to be without Charity, to be Christians in name only....[13]

It is evident from listening to these saints that we must love with our whole selves. We cannot love halfway, or without putting our heart into it. Jesus wants a love which, as Luke says, moves us to compassion (see Lk. 10:33). We must give ourselves totally to our neighbor and receive him or her into our hearts.

If a neighbor wrongs us, we must not answer evil with evil but "overcome evil with good" (Rom. 12:21). We must do good to everyone, especially those who share our faith. If we do this, love will more easily become reciprocal. And this mutual love will be of benefit to our brothers and sisters without faith, because it is a witness of God.

Charity, which tends toward reciprocity, has the power to build the Christian community. Paul writes that "love builds up" (1 Cor. 8:1), which means that with Christian love we build up the community. And this was the experience of the Movement at its birth: from isolated members we became a community. It is evident that Christian love was at work in the first Focolarine.

Human beings are not instruments for loving God

Someone might think that in Christianity people could be used as a means for loving God. But that is not so. The theologian Emile Mersch writes:

> Man is an end in himself, an absolute and ultimate value, and mere natural philanthropy can arrive at love for him because of his intrinsic greatness. Could the Charity of Christ be less human...and fail to discover in man more than a mere means for loving God....
>
> A child can doubtless be happy and proud to be loved for his parents' sake. But this is because he *is* in a way his parents.... Yet this should definitely not be the only love he encounters; if it were, he would soon feel not loved, but ignored....
>
> Love is truly directed to the person himself. It does not pass through him in order to go beyond. What would it be seeking beyond the person?

From the moment that the Word became flesh, became one with us (Gal. 3:28), we no longer seek God only in far-off heaven, but within each human being as well. He is there...as the inner source of life and divinization.[14]

Moreover, the *Pastoral Constitution on the Church in the Modern World* of Vatican II says that "by His incarnation the Son of God has united Himself in some fashion with every human being."[15]

And Catherine of Siena explains what becomes of those who live charity, by revealing to us what the "gentle and loving Word" told her:

...looking at the beauty that I have given the soul, creating it in my image and likeness, observe those who are clothed in the wedding garment of Charity, adorned with many real and true virtues, and united to me through love. If you should ask me: "Who are they?" I would answer: "They are another me...."[16]

Charity, therefore, divinizes us, makes us sharers in Christ's divinity.

Abbreviations

Abbott   Walter M. Abbott, editor. *The Documents of Vatican II.* New York, 1966.

PG   J.P. Migne. *Patrologiae Cursus Completus Series Graeca.* 162 Vols. Paris, 1857-1866.

PL   J.P. Migne. *Patrologiae Cursus Completus Series Latina.* 221 Vols. Paris, 1844-1864.

Notes

Chapter 1

1. Claus Westermann, *Genesis* I/1 (Neukirchen, 1974) pp. 217-218.
2. Irenaeus, *Against Heresies* IV.20.1, in *The Ante-Nicene Fathers* (Grand Rapids, 1969), Vol. I, pp. 487-488 (*PG* 7, 1032).
3. Gregory of Nyssa, *De hom. opif.* 5 (*PG* 44, 137).
4. John Chrysostom, Homily III Concerning the Statues, in *The Nicene and Post-Nicene Fathers* (Grand Rapids, 1956), Vol. IX, p. 362; *PG* 49, 57.
5. Origen, *In Gen. hom.* XIII.4 (*PG* 12, 234).
6. Augustine, *On the Psalms,* translated by S. Hebgin and F. Corrigan (Westminster, Md.,

117

1960), Vol. I, p. 47; *PL* 36, 81.

7. Irenaeus, *Against Heresies* V.10.1, in *The Ante-Nicene Fathers* Vol. I (Grand Rapids, 1969) p. 536; *PG* 7, 1147-1148.

8. Pope Paul VI, Address of December 8, 1965 at the close of the Second Vatican Council, in *The Teachings of the Second Vatican Council* (Westminster, Md., 1966) p. 606.

9. Pope Paul VI, Apostolic Exhortation *Marialis Cultus*, par. 57, in *The Teachings of Pope Paul VI*, Vol. 7 (Vatican, 1974) p. 428.

10. Gottfried Hierzenberger in *Praktisches Bibellexikon*, ed. Anton Grabner—Haider (Freiburg, 1977), col. 740.

11. Walther Eichrodt, *Theology of the Old Testament* (London, 1961), Vol. I, p. 365.

12. Notker Füglister, "Afferrati da Jahwè" in J. Schreiner *et. al., Parola e Messaggio* (Bari, 1970), p. 222.

13. Otto Kaiser, *Isaiah 1-12: A Commentary* (Philadelphia, 1972) p. 16.

14. See Claus Westermann, *Isaiah 40-66: A Commentary* (London, 1969) pp. 336-337.

Chapter 2

1. Cf. S. Légasse, *Jésus et l'enfant* (Paris, 1969), pp. 72-75.

2. Stanislas Lyonnet, S.J., "The Presence of Christ and His Spirit in Man" in *Concilium* 50 (1969) p. 101.

3. F.X. Durrwell, *La resurrection de Jésus mystère de salut,* 10th (entirely revised) edition (Paris, 1976), pp. 169-170; cf. English translation by Rosemary Sheed of the 2nd French edition: *The Resurrection: A Biblical Study* (New York, 1960) pp. 216-217.

4. M.-J. Lagrange, *Evangile selon St. Jean,* 5th ed. (Paris, 1936) p. 389.

5. In this book we have used a few words from the original Italian which have become proper names in the Focolare Movement all over the world. The name "Focolare" itself is the Italian word for hearth or fireplace around which people gather as a family. It refers to a community of consecrated people who live the spirituality of the Movement, and it has also come to signify the Movement as a whole. A woman living in a women's Focolare is a "Focolarina" (plural "Focolarine") and a man living in a men's community is a "Focolarino" (plural "Focolarini").

Chapter 3

1. John Chrysostom, *Homilies on the Gospel of*

Matthew, 88,3 (*PG* 58, 778).

2. Leo the Great, *Sermons,* 10,2 (*PL* 54, 165).
3. John Chrysostom, *Matthew,* 50,4 (*PG* 58, 508-509).
4. Cyprian, *The Dress of Virgins,* 11 (**PL** 4, 461-462).
5. Ambrose, *De Tobia,* 16,55 (*PL* 14, 781).
6. Ambrose, *Letters,* 21,33 (*PL* 16, 1017).
7. Augustine, *On the Psalms,* 33,3,6 (*PL* 36, 388).
8. Curé of Ars, *Pensieri* in *Scritti scelti* (Rome, 1975) p. 83.
9. Curé of Ars in *Scritti scelti,* p. 83.
10. Bonaventure, *Legenda Minor,* 7.
11. Raymond of Capua, *The Life of St. Catherine of Siena,* tr. by George Lamb (New York, 1960) pp. 121-124 (abridged).
12. M. Auclair, *La parola a San Vincenzo de Paoli* (Rome, 1971) p. 132.
13. Bonaventure, *Legenda Maior* 1,5 in *The Soul's Journey to God—The Tree of Life—The Life of St. Francis,* tr. by E. Cousins (New York, 1978) pp. 188-189.
14. Bonaventure, *Legenda Maior* 8,5 in Cousins, p. 254.
15. *Insegnamenti di Paolo VI,* II (Vatican, 1965) p. 1110.
16. *Insegnamenti di Paolo VI,* II (Vatican, 1965) p. 1178.

17. *Insegnamenti di Paolo VI*, III (Vatican, 1966) pp. 1219-1220.
18. Pope John Paul I, General audience of September 27, 1978, in *The Pope Speaks* 23 (1978) p. 328.
19. See Chapter 2, Note 5.

Chapter 4

1. See P. Rossano, "What the II Vatican Council has taught regarding non-Christians," *Christ to the World* 12 (1967), pp. 428-436.
2. *Ad Gentes: Decree on the Church's Missionary Activity*, Art. 4, Abbott, p. 587.
3. *Nostra Aetate: Declaration on the Relationship of the Church to Non-Christian Religions*, Art. 2, Abbott, p. 662.
4. *Ad Gentes*, Art. 9, Abbott, pp. 595-596.
5. *Nostra Aetate*, Art. 2, Abbott, p. 662.
6. *A.G.*, Art. 11, Abbott, p. 598.
7. Justin Martyr, *Second Apology*, 13 (*PG* 6, 465-468).
8. *A.G.*, Art. 18, Abbott, p. 607.
9. *A.G.*, Art. 3, Abbott, p. 586.
10. *Lumen Gentium: Dogmatic Constitution on the Church*, Art. 16, Abbott, p. 35.
11. See *A.G.*, Art. 9, Abbott, pp. 595-596.
12. See *Nostra Aetate*, Art. 2, Abbott, pp. 662-663.

13. See P. Rossano (above. Ch. 4, note 1).

14. *A.G.*, Art. 11, Abbott, p. 598.

15. *A.G.*, Art. 22, Abbott, pp. 612-613.

16. *Sacrosanctum Concilium: Constitution on the Sacred Liturgy*, Art. 37, Abbott, p. 151.

17. See: *A.G.*, Art. 12, 41, Abbott, pp. 598, 628; *N.A.*, Art. 2, 5, Abbott, pp. 661, 667; *Unitatis Redintegratio: Decree on Ecumenism*, Art. 12, Abbott, p. 354; *Apostolicam Actuositatem: Decree on the Apostolate of the Laity*, Art. 27, Abbott, p. 515.

18. *L.G.*, Art. 16, Abbott, pp. 34-35.

19. See *Cristiani e musulmani,* ed. by Secretariat for non-Christians (Bologna, 1970), pp. 36-39.

20. Quotes from the Koran taken from *The Koran,* translated by N.J. Dawood (New York, 1974).

21. See *Cristiani e musulmani,* pp. 71-73.

22. See *Cristiani e musulmani,* pp. 30-32.

23. See R. Arnaldey, "La mystique musulmane" in *La mystique et les mystiques* (Paris, 1975), pp. 579-580.

24. D. Spada, "Induismo" in *Le grandi religioni del mondo* (Rome, 1977), pp. 97-99. Scripture quotes here and in note 26 taken from *Hindu Scriptures,* translated by R.C. Zaehner (London, 1966).

25. P. Rossano, *L'uomo e la religione* (Fossano, 1968).

26. H. Le Saux, "Sagesse Hindoue Mystique Chrétienne du védanta à la Trinité (Paris, 1965) pp. 217-218; cf. the revised English edition: Abhishiktananda [H. Le Saux], *Saccidananda: A Christian Approach to Advaitic Experience* (Delhi, 1974) p. 158.

27. H. Le Saux, French ed., pp. 218-219; English ed., p. 159.

28. See M. Dhavamony, "La ricerca della salvezza nell'Induismo" in *La ricerca della salvezza* (Fossano, 1969), p. 103.

29. *N.A.*, Art. 2, Abbott, pp. 661-662.

30. See J. Masson, "Il bene e il male nel buddismo" in *Il bene e il male nelle religioni* (Fossano, 1970), pp. 100-101.

31. See G. Shirieda, "Il buddismo" in *Le religioni non cristiane nel Vaticano II* (Turin, 1966), pp. 144-145.

32. G. Shirieda, pp. 146-148; see J. Masson, pp. 105-106.

33. *Gaudium et Spes: Pastoral Constitution on the Church in the Modern World,* Art. 22, Abbott, pp. 221-222.

34. *Gaudium et Spes,* Art. 22, Abbott, p. 221; see *L.G.,* Art. 16, Abbott, p. 35.

35. See P. Rossano, "What the II Vatican Council has taught regarding non-Christians."

36. *A.G.,* Art. 3, Abbott, p. 112.

37. *G.S.,* Art. 16, Abbott, pp. 213-214.
38. *A.G.,* Art. 12, Abbott, p. 599.
39. See *G.S.,* Art. 16, Abbott, p. 214.
40. *G.S.,* Art. 36, Abbott, p. 234.
41. *Lumen Gentium,* Art. 16, Abbott, p. 35.
42. *Traduction Oecumenique de la Bible* (Paris, 1977), note z, p. 297.
43. *L.G.,* Art. 48, Abbott, p. 79.

Chapter 5

1. Catherine of Siena, *Dialogo,* 69, in *Il messaggio di Santa Caterina da Siena dottore della Chiesa* (Rome, 1970) pp. 689-690.
2. Igino Giordani is a well-known writer, journalist, and university professor. He has also been a member of the Italian Parliament. In 1949, he became the first married Focolarino.
3. Gregory the Great, *Morals on the Book of Job,* 7,28 (*PL* 75, 780-781).
4. Isidore of Seville, *Sententiae,* II,3,7 (*PL* 83,603).
5. Curé of Ars, *Scritti scelti* (Rome, 1975) p. 114.
6. John of the Cross, quoted in P. Descouvemont, *Sainte Thérèse de l'Enfant Jésus et son prochain* (Paris, 1962) p. 209.
7. E. Dhanis, "Le message évangélique de l'amour et l'unité de la communauté humaine," *Nouvelle Revue Théologique,* 92 (1970) pp. 186-188.

8. "Amore di Dio e amore del prossimo," in *La Civiltà Cattolica*, 3053 (1977) pp. 346-347.
9. See *Civiltà Cattolica*, 3053 (1977) pp. 351-352.
10. See *Civiltà Cattolica*, 3053 (1977) pp. 349-350.
11. Leo the Great, *Sermons*, 45,3 (*PL* 54, 290).
12. *Scritti scelti*, p. 117.
13. M. Auclair, *La parola a San Vincenzo de' Paoli* (Rome, 1971) pp. 354-355.
14. Emile Mersch, *Morale et Corps Mystique*, 3rd ed. (Paris, 1949) pp. 146-147.
15. *G.S.*, Art. 22, Abbott, pp. 220-221.
16. Catherine of Siena, *Dialogo*, 1, in *Il messaggio*, p. 243.

COLLECTION OF THE WORKS OF CHIARA LUBICH

The Eucharist

This work, in a contemporary approach, brings together much of the wisdom of the Church. The Eucharist comes across here as a prolongation of Christ's incarnation through the centuries, a possibility for everyone to form "one body" with Christ and with all men.

93 pp. ISBN 0-911782-30-3   Paper $1.95

"Jesus In the Midst"

In this collection of talks the author examines the spiritual presence of Christ in the community. The treatment of the topic rests on a most authentic tradition of the Church, reaching back to the Church Fathers. It is not just an outgrowth of speculative thought, however, but the fruit of a genuine Christian experience based on Scripture. This is what makes it convincing, timely, and attractive for the Christian today.

80 pp. ISBN 0-911782-26-5   Paper $1.50

The Word of Life

This book is a concise and straightforward presentation of how to live the "word of life," that is to say, the Gospel. It contains four brief talks given by Chiara Lubich to the members of the Focolare Movement. For those who look to the Gospel as the foundation for radical change, these pages are packed with new ideas for action.

95 pp. ISBN 0-911782-25-7   Paper $1.15

When Our Love is Charity

In this book Chiara Lubich deals in particular with going to God through our brother and being of one heart and of one mind in a pluralistic society. Something new, showing the inexhaustible resources of the Holy Spirit.

82 pp. 2nd printing ISBN 0-911782-24-9   Paper $1.15

That All Men Be One

This is the inspiring account of the events which surround the birth of the Focolare Movement, and the vast results that they have produced. Taking a stand against the hatred and absurdity of the second world war, putting in the balance their very lives, a small group of young girls rediscovered the truth of the Gospel with effects that were to motivate hundreds of thousands of people around the world to work for the solidarity of the human race.

105 pp. 4th printing ISBN 0-911782-21-4   Paper $1.95

Meditations

This book is a collection of meditations. Even though they originally came to life on different days and even over different years, Chiara Lubich's individual insights are linked together by one basic theme: God is Love.

148 pp. 2nd printing ISBN 0-911782-20-6   Paper $1.50

A Little 'Harmless' Manifesto

In this powerful essay, Chiara Lubich expresses some of the ideas which are at the core of the spirituality of the Focolare Movement.

52 pp. ISBN 0-911782-17-6   Paper $0.95

It's A Whole New Scene

High-powered, brief thoughts for youth attracted by Jesus Christ. The book can set a fast pace in one's growth toward God and people.

67 pp. ISBN 0-911782-01-X   paper $0.75

Servants of All

Originally presented as a series of talks on theology and spirituality to members of the Focolare Movement, the chapters of this book are intended to highlight the presence of Christ in the hierarchy of the Church. They constitute a harmonious and unified whole, characterized by a warm and lively presentation, serious theological content, clarity of expression, and an all pervading love for the Church.

"The present volume, small in size but great in content, should not be read with the superficial curiosity of a hurried tourist, but rather with the attitude of a person who is seriously searching for the truth that can enlighten one's mind, inflame one's heart, and bring one to the fullness of life" (Federico Didonet, Bishop of Rio Grande, Brazil).

167 pp. ISBN 0-911782-05-2   Paper $2.50

**OTHER BOOKS PUBLISHED
BY NEW CITY PRESS
206 Skillman Avenue, Brooklyn, NY 11211**

Focolare: After 30 Years
Sergius C. Lorit & Nuzzo M. Grimaldi

This book is an attempt to provide some information about the Focolare Movement. It is not intended to give a complete view of the subject. For the Focolare Movement, as a movement of renewal, is continually growing, expanding and developing, albeit from the strong and solid spirituality which lies at its heart.

The book contains interviews with a number of people with responsibility in the Movement at an international level, beginning with Chiara Lubich, the foundress and president. It also describes some of the activities of the Movement throughout the world.

268 pp., 136 illustrations ISBN 0-911782-27-3   Paper $4.50

Reaching for More
Pascal Foresi

The chapters in this book treat various Gospel passages in all their unsettling and fascinating reality. The author's style is informal because the book is a collection of "conversations" he had with his friends (the Focolarini). The biblical foundation is as solid as it is helpful. The author draws conclusions that can enlighten the intellect and warm the heart. This is indeed a book for modern times. It is sure to have an impact on those Christians who want to be authentic without compromise.

Fr. Foresi is the author of several theological and spiritual publications. He has contributed to the birth and development of the "Focolare" Movement. He did his philosophical and theological studies at the Gregorian and Lateran Universities in Rome. He is the head of the Department of Theological Research at the International Institute for the Apostolate of the Laity (Loppiano, Florence, Italy).

208 pp. ISBN 0-911782-04-4   Paper $1.50

Celibacy Put to the Gospel Test
Pascal Foresi

The title describes the content. The subject is one many responsible Christians will want to ponder. At last someone dares to cover this topic in a way that can be understood by the layman as well as the religious.

34 pp. ISBN 0-911782-16-8   Paper $0.50

The Gospel in Action
C. Miner

These are true stories. We see a mother, an office worker, a doctor, and others, living and working in circumstances similar to our own. Their deceptively modest experiences under normal working conditions, demonstrate the possibility of relationships among men which are humanly warm and complete but also somehow divine.

153 pp. ISBN 0-911782-23-0   Paper $1.50

Me Too, Forever
C. Miner

These experiences have been written down from first-hand accounts. It is typical of young people to believe in an ideal totally and to dedicate themselves to it completely. The ideal that is revealed in each of these stories is truly worthy of an absolute response, because the Ideal is God Himself.

119 pp. ISBN 0-911782-22-2   Paper $1.50

The Difficult Role of a Father
Spartaco Lucarini

A brief, wise book on learning the art that has eluded so many fathers, who have not been able to maintain open and trusting relationships with their children during the teenage years. The author, journalist Spartaco Lucarini, himself a father of five, bases his book on the experience of many fathers, along with the experience of their sons and daughters. He vividly portrays the tragic dead ends into which many fathers stray by either becoming authoritarian or physically and emotionally absent and uninvolved. He offers the reader a clear alternative, however, by showing a way of succeeding as a father. The book—which offers a role to the parent without a role—also discusses discipline and sex education.

ISBN 0-911782-32-X

Paper $2.25

The Difficult Role of a Mother
Anne Marie Zanzucchi

This book is based on the down-to-earth experiences of a mother of five, who sees the mother's role as the round-the-clock educator of her children. Every mother can relate to the practical solutions she finds for everyday situations—solutions that always begin with transforming her own attitude into one of love. Her practical, yet penetrating approach to the problems of family life will both reassure and inspire the mother of today.

ISBN 0-911782-33-8

Paper $2.25

My Child and God
Religious Education in the Family
Anne Marie Zanzucchi

The method of religious education explored in this book is rooted in reality, in the experience of the author and a group of parents whom she interviews. They speak honestly and freely about the difficulty and the success they have encountered introducing their children to God, to prayer, to Jesus and Mary, to the Scriptures, the examination of conscience, the sacraments, suffering, and death. The goal of this method is to contribute to the formation of a human being who believes in the love of God and who has learned to love.

99 pp. ISBN 0-911782-31-1   Paper $2.25

Sketches of the Universe
Piero Pasolini

In this book the reader is drawn by the author into the infinitesimal world of the atom at the very heart of matter, until he reaches the point where matter itself seems to be swallowed up in abysmal nothingness and events take place in billionths of a second. Then he is led toward the ultimate expression of material creation—to man, who himself material, by a marvelous process shares in the realm of the spiritual.

This readable, swift-moving, yet rigorously scientific book will provide readers, whether or not they are qualified in this field, with enjoyment and thought-provoking inspiration.

Piero Pasolini is a physicist who has published in six languages many articles and books on the philosophical implications of scientific discovery.

248 pp. ISBN 0-911782-15-X   Paper $1.95

Everybody's Pope: John XXIII
Sergius C. Lorit

The story of the Pope who taught the world how to smile again. The author recounts the Pope's life in a popular style while not diminishing his immense moral and religious stature. A book to acquaint oneself with or keep warm the memory of this man who left so deep a mark on contemporary history.

230 pp. ISBN 0-911782-06-0

Paper $1.00

Charles de Foucauld: the Silent Witness
Sergius C. Lorit

Few today have not heard of the once flamboyant French officer who became the poorest among the poor in the heart of the Sahara to be closer to Christ. An intriguing biography that promises the reader light for his personal life.

174 pp. ISBN 0-911782-29-X

Paper $2.50

The Last Writings of Reginald Garrigou-Lagrange

The book is a serious guide for all those who want to develop themselves in the spiritual life. Garrigou-Lagrange was a master, an expert in directing people. These are his precious last writings summarizing his outstanding career as a man who knew men.

224 pp. ISBN 0-911782-12-5

Cloth $5.95

No longer the property of
Conejos County Library

Conejos County Library
La Jara, Colorado 81140

My father pulled his chair close to mine. "Do you know how much I love you?" he said.

"Yes. I think so."

"Well then, if you know that, don't break my heart. And don't break your mother's heart, either. Your fella's a *loser*, Rita, an all-time loser. He'll be writing that book for the rest of his life. And he will never, ever, support you."

And then—as though a light had gone on in my head—I saw the whole thing. And the clarity of it was astounding. I saw that my father was right, but that I was right too. Yes, Arnold would probably never finish his book, and yes, I would have to support him for the rest of my life, and yes, Arnold Bromberg was a character and an oddball. *But what the hell was wrong with that?* What did it matter *who* brought money into the house, and what did it matter where we lived or what we owned? The point—the goddam point of the whole thing—was that Arnold and I were not just committed to each other, we were also committed to ourselves.

BARBARA WERSBA is the author of more than seventeen books for young readers, including *Fat: A Love Story* and *Love Is the Crooked Thing,* both available in Laurel-Leaf editions. She lives in Sag Harbor, New York.

BEAUTIFUL
LOSERS

ALSO AVAILABLE IN LAUREL-LEAF BOOKS:

FAT: A LOVE STORY, *Barbara Wersba*
LOVE IS THE CROOKED THING, *Barbara Wersba*
SEX EDUCATION, *Jenny Davis*
GOOD-BYE AND KEEP COLD, *Jenny Davis*
THE OUTSIDERS, *S. E. Hinton*
THAT WAS THEN, THIS IS NOW, *S. E. Hinton*
RUMBLE FISH, *S. E. Hinton*
TEX, *S. E. Hinton*
TAMING THE STAR RUNNER, *S. E. Hinton*
THOSE SUMMER GIRLS I NEVER MET, *Richard Peck*

QUANTITY SALES

Most Dell books are available at special quantity discounts when purchased in bulk by corporations, organizations, and special-interest groups. Custom imprinting or excerpting can also be done to fit special needs. For details write: Dell Publishing, 666 Fifth Avenue, New York, NY 10103. Attn.: Special Sales Department.

INDIVIDUAL SALES

Are there any Dell books you want but cannot find in your local stores? If so, you can order them directly from us. You can get any Dell book in print. Simply include the book's title, author, and ISBN number if you have it, along with a check or money order (no cash can be accepted) for the full retail price plus $2.00 to cover shipping and handling. Mail to: Dell Readers Service, P.O. Box 5057, Des Plaines, IL 60017.

BARBARA WERSBA

BEAUTIFUL
LOSERS

LAUREL-LEAF BOOKS

LAUREL-LEAF BOOKS bring together under a single imprint outstanding works of fiction and nonfiction particularly suitable for young adult readers, both in and out of the classroom. Charles F. Reasoner, Professor Emeritus of Children's Literature and Reading, New York University, is consultant to this series.

Published by
Dell Publishing
a division of
Bantam Doubleday Dell Publishing Group, Inc.
666 Fifth Avenue
New York, New York 10103

Copyright © 1988 by Barbara Wersba

All rights reserved. No part of this book may be reproduced or transmitted in any form or by any means, electronic or mechanical, including photocopying, recording or by any information storage and retrieval system, without the written permission of the Publisher, except where permitted by law. For information address Harper & Row Junior Books, New York, New York 10022.

The trademark Laurel-Leaf Library® is registered in the U.S. Patent and Trademark Office.

ISBN: 0-440-20580-8

RL: 5.3

Reprinted by arrangement with Harper & Row, Publishers

Printed in the United States of America

March 1990

10 9 8 7 6 5 4 3 2 1

KRI

Conejos County Library
La Jara, Colorado 81140

BEAUTIFUL
LOSERS

I

DO YOU KNOW WHAT my mother used to say to me when I was little? "You can be a cucumber all your life, but once you become a pickle there's no turning back." The thing that drove me crazy was that I never knew what she meant by that. Did she mean that it was safer to be a pure and virginal cucumber than a world-weary pickle? Or did she mean that once you become a pickle, it is downhill all the way? Pickles are shriveled and sour. Cucumbers have a certain optimism.

I never did find out what she meant. But during the summer that I turned eighteen, she began saying it again—only this time, she said it ominously. "You know, Rita," she would say in that tone of voice I used to hate, "you can be a cucumber all your life, but once you become a *pickle* there's no turning back."

"So what's wrong with pickles?" I would ask, trying to be lighthearted. "They're cute."

"You know what I mean, Rita."

"But Mom, I don't!"

"Well then, think about it," she said. "Think about your future."

The thing she was referring to was a situation I had been involved in for the past two years, a situation which was now coming to a head, and which caused her and my father a lot of grief. Namely, the fact that I was in love with a man who was twice my age and who had never earned a living. Arnold Bromberg.

I had met Arnold the summer I turned sixteen, in my hometown of Sag Harbor, New York, and once I realized that I loved him the whole world changed for me. You see, I am a very short, fat person—five foot three, as a matter of fact—and to say that I have had an inferiority complex for most of my life is like saying that the Empire State Building is rather tall. For most of my life I have felt like a klutz, a fatty, an oddball, a failure, and a freak. But then I met Arnold.

4

It was the summer of my sixteenth birthday, and, as usual, I needed a summer job. So I answered an ad in the local paper—for a deliveryperson to deliver something called *Arnold's Cheesecake*—and the man placing the ad turned out to be Arnold Bromberg. For reasons that are still unclear to me, he fell in love with me right away. I, on the other hand, took longer to fall in love with him because his virtues were not immediately apparent.

What a fool I was! Because, let me tell you, men like Arnold do not surface in the ocean of one's life on a daily basis. Men like Arnold, as a matter of fact, are as rare as hen's teeth. Getting together with Arnold, however, was like climbing the Matterhorn. Crags and precipices.

To begin with, he had a great many scruples about sleeping with me because I was a virgin. But eventually we made love, and the whole thing was so beautiful that neither of us could believe it. Then my parents found out about the affair and tried to break it up. I mean, they dragged me into family counseling with a shrink named Mrs. Perlman, and Arnold even came to one of the sessions too. As far as my parents were concerned, he was nothing more than a drifter—a kind of aging hippie in a business suit.

OK. I'll grant you that Arnold had been through

five or six different professions—that cheesecake business being one of them. But he was also a man who could play the organ brilliantly, who was writing a book on Bach, and who had almost completed a Ph.D. in English Literature. He loved nature and cooking and poetry, was deeply into metaphysics, and had moved to Sag Harbor from Kansas merely because he had seen the words "Sag Harbor" on a map and fallen in love with them.

Arnold's father was a minister, and he had grown up in a very sheltered environment. Like me, he was an only child. It wasn't that he was a loser, as my father persisted in calling him. It was that he was an idealist—a man who lived for beauty, and who was sweet and gentle into his very soul. A big, tousled teddy bear of a man who wore glasses and had sea-green eyes and brown curly hair. A man who went about in sneakers and old business suits, and whose overcoat was so ancient it looked like an antique. Look, I'll admit this to you—I had thought he was a little weird myself. I mean, in the beginning he talked a lot to me about the universe and God, and how Right Action is always taking place, no matter how crummy things seem. So of course I thought he was a little bent. Then, as we drew closer and closer, I saw that he wasn't bent at all. He was a genius.

6

"Genius?" my father said to me. "What kind of genius wears sneakers in January? What kind of genius can't even pay his rent? You want geniuses, I'll find you one. But this character is for the birds."

I had met Arnold in June, and by December we were lovers. And our lovemaking was so profound that it overwhelmed us both. During the first weeks of the affair we had sex so often that I got a little worried, rushed off to a doctor who was sympathetic to such things, and got myself some birth control pills. Then my mother found the pills. Then she and my father dragged me into therapy. And then—Arnold Bromberg walked out.

The incredible thing is that he agreed with them. He *was* too old for me, he declared, and it was true that he had never earned a decent living. Everything my parents had said was correct, declared Arnold. And so he split.

Do you know where he went, that winter? No, not back to Kansas, and not even to New York City. To Zurich, Switzerland. Wanting to get as far away from me as possible, he thrust himself into the heart of Europe, traveling from city to city and eventually winding up in Zurich. Once settled there, he proceeded to take organ lessons at the Fraumunster cathedral and continued to work on his book. He sent me postcards, and all of the postcards

7

said that he loved me. And I, who had lost forty pounds for Arnold—forty, count them, forty—went back to eating like a junkie.

There is something you don't know about me yet. And this is the fact that I am a very determined person. Maybe it comes from my having been such an outsider all of my life, but let me tell you, when I decide to do something, I *do* it. So what I did was—I went to Zurich. Yes. For five days. And the logistics of this were so complicated that I am not going to bore you with them. All I want to say here is that I told my parents I would be staying in New York City that week, with a friend, and then I took myself off on a wide-bodied jet to Zurich. I, Rita Formica, who had never been anywhere before—except twice to Florida—took herself off to Europe. The money for the trip came from a local woman, a rich person named Doris Morris. But the courage for the trip came from me.

Gray skies and church bells, swans and cobbled streets, the River Limmat winding like a ribbon through the heart of the Old Town—and me and Arnold Bromberg in a small hotel, locked in each other's arms. Traffic along the lakefront, and bells ringing, and Arnold and I kissing as though we were going to die the next day. I'm not kidding you. I really went to Zurich for five days and my parents never knew about it. But the thing was,

8

Arnold would not come back to America with me. Our lovemaking, our whole connection, was so deep and so miraculous that I couldn't believe the words when he finally said them. But he was not coming back. He wanted to stay in Switzerland and write his book and study the organ. He wanted to become *Zurichoise*.

Just thinking about all this makes me want to cry. Because the disappointment I felt was so terrible that it almost killed me. I mean, I knew—and he knew—that there were no two people on earth more right for each other than we were, and yet he wouldn't come back to the States. And then I realized something profound. Arnold Bromberg was a person who did not want to be trapped. By anyone. He was a confirmed bachelor who had no intention of getting married because he liked his freedom too much. His freedom to be poor, and travel, and write a book on the life of Johann Sebastian Bach. The thing he was afraid of was responsibility—just like my father had always said.

You may be wondering how we resolved it, Arnold and I. The answer is that we didn't. He stayed in Zurich and I came back to America, but between us, invisibly, a question mark remained. It wasn't over, I told myself, because I would love him for the rest of my life. It just wasn't over.

2

SAG HARBOR, where I live, is a part of something on the east end of Long Island that is called the Hamptons—and these Hamptons are just a lot of little towns near the ocean that have been turned into summer resorts. Sag Harbor, which was once a whaling port and then a factory town, is the one shabby Hampton in the group—but I've always lived here, and so I like it. My father, who owns Tony's Auto Repair over on Clarence Street, was born here, and my mother moved here when she was a little girl. Not that that makes us natives—because you have to go back for many generations to be considered a native—but we do think of this as our hometown. My mother worked here in real estate for a long time, and my dad is a friendly type who knows everyone in town. I once overheard my aunt telling my mother that she—Mom, I mean—had married beneath her, but this made my mother very angry. It's true that she did have two years of college, while Dad is a high school dropout, but I know that she loves him. The thing is, after twenty years of marriage they are bored with each other. They like their life, and they like their routine—but the boredom of the whole thing is terrible. Most evenings they sit together in the living room like statues, watching television—and when they go out

10

together to a restaurant, they seem glazed. I'm sure you've seen married couples like them—sitting across the table from each other but not speaking. Each of them a million miles away.

At any rate, it was June, I had just graduated from Peterson High School—and I was about to confront the biggest mistake I had ever made. Which was that I had lied to both my parents about going to college. *They* thought that I was off to Hofstra University in the fall—because, indeed, I had been accepted there. What they didn't know was that I had turned Hofstra down.

And also Stony Brook, where I had been accepted too. And also Southampton College. And also a tiny outfit upstate that wanted me to join their ranks so fervently that they had offered me a full scholarship. I had turned everyone down because I had other plans for my life. The trouble is, I had lied about it.

Poor Mom. There she was that June, haunting every shopping mall on Long Island, picking out clothes for me—for college—and there *I* was, trailing miserably behind her, sunk in the knowledge that I wasn't going anywhere. I had written dignified, formal letters to every one of these places turning them down. And why? Because I had decided to become a writer.

You are probably thinking that college is not

exactly an impediment to a person who wants to become a writer. But the thing is, I wanted to be a writer *now*. Not a student, not a novice, but a professional writer who earned money. And I was positive I could do this, because I already had a writing job. In May, I had become sole author of the "Hospital News" newsletter at Hampton Hospital. Not exactly the same as penning *War and Peace*, but what the hell. A job is a job.

It was Arnold who had revealed to me that I should be a writer—the summer I turned sixteen—and the minute this happened, I knew he was correct. I had the soul of a writer and the temperament of a writer, the only problem being that I did not know what to write. Fiction? Autobiography? History? Plays, maybe. Or maybe poems. It was a complex problem, because I couldn't seem to find the right form—whereas Arnold, of course, was writing his book on Bach. Biography, with a metaphysical twist. Genius as a revelation of the infinite.

I don't mean to be glib about this, because I had read parts of Arnold's book and had found them beautiful. But then, Arnold was very well educated—as I was not—and could quote Yeats and T. S. Eliot by the hour. An amateur actor, who had once acted with a Shakespeare company in the Middle West, he had a beautiful, resonant voice that absolutely hypnotized me.

On the plane coming back Anyway, I father l struck me that I should write Arnold Bromberg and me. A few I had tried to write a historical roma boiler—to get the money to go to Zuric had failed at this, and the agent for whom was writing the book, Doris Morris, had felt so sorry for me that she had loaned me money for the trip. But coming back on the plane it occurred to me that I might be able to write a *real* romance—the story of me and Arnold. I would call it *All the Slow Dances*.

Good title, don't you think? It came from the fact that the one and only time Arnold and I had ever danced together—to the radio—he had confessed that he could only dance to slow music, old-fashioned tunes like "Deep Purple" or "My Funny Valentine." This had been an impediment to him in high school, he explained, this desire to fox-trot when everyone else was doing the hustle or the shambala, or whatever. *Un original* in every way, Arnold Bromberg had gone through four years of high school dancing slow.

The point is this. I *needed* that book. To sort things out for me. To make my parents—and Arnold—realize that Arnold and I belonged together. It wasn't just a book, it was a mission. The new purpose of my life.

It was the middle of June now, my
had sent my tuition and room-and-board
checks off to Hofstra, and I still hadn't told my
parents that I had turned Hofstra down. And with
each passing day I was getting more and more scared.
I knew I had to tell them what I had done, but
couldn't seem to find the right moment, the right
setting. Then the checks my father had sent to Hofstra were returned to him, with a covering letter,
and the mud hit the fan. As the expression goes.

It was the middle of the day, a bright June day,
and my father should have been at work. Instead,
I came home from doing some errands and found
him and my mother waiting for me in the living
room. And, let me tell you, the look on their faces
was not reassuring. My mother looked stunned.
My father looked insane.

"Rita!" he began. "Come in here! On the double!"

I hurried into the living room. "Yes?" I said.
"What is it? What's happened?"

"I'll tell you what's happened," said my father,
waving a piece of paper at me. "I have a letter here
from Hofstra saying that you turned them down.
Hofstra University! What the hell have you done?"

"Well . . ." I said.

"Who are you to turn down Hofstra Univer-

14

sity?" my father screamed. "Who do you think you are?"

I sighed and sank down on the sofa. "I'm sorry I didn't tell you sooner. That was a mistake."

"What have you done, you nincompoop? Did you turn down all of the others too?"

"Yes," I said.

"But Rita, *why*?" said my mother.

"Because I don't want to go," I said calmly. "I want to be a writer."

"And writers don't go to college?" my father said. "Writers don't get an education?"

"I'm not going. And you know very well that I already have a writing job."

"You call that a job? Writing a hospital newsletter? Writing about new toilet facilities on the fourth floor?"

"I don't just write about toilet facilities," I said, trying to muster some dignity. "That's very unfair."

"You fool," said my father. "You've blown the whole thing."

"Rita," said my mother, "on the day you were born, your father opened a special bank account, and what was this bank account for? For you. For your education. And he has put something into this account, regularly, for the past eighteen years. He

15

never saved any money for himself, just for you. Only for you."

"Well," I said, "I never asked him to do that. Now did I?"

My father sat down next to me on the sofa. "You are going to write Hofstra University and tell them that it was all a mistake. You are going to tell them that you'll be there in September."

"I'm sorry. I can't do that."

My father, whose bark is worse than his bite, looked like he might cry. He has a slight drinking problem and cries very easily.

"Daddy," I said, taking his hand, "it's *my* life we're talking about. Not yours, not Mom's, but mine. And I simply do not want to go to college."

"Ah, what do you know," he said wearily. "At eighteen, what does anyone know? At eighteen, I wanted to be a racing car driver. Big deal."

On and on. But I'll tell you something. It occurred to me that afternoon that my father would have been happier had he *been* a racing car driver. He has an absolute passion for cars, so what did he become? A mechanic, and then the owner of an auto repair shop. Every Saturday afternoon, during the racing season, he sits glued to the television set—and there is a look on his face that almost breaks my heart. Because in his imagination he, Tony Formica, is in one of those cars too. Strapped

16

down into some sleek little Porsche and going around the track at 150 miles an hour. Sad, sad.

What happened was that the whole thing became a stalemate. They wouldn't give in, and I wouldn't give in—and every time the subject of college came up, my father would say, "We'll talk about it in a few weeks. You'll change your mind." But of course I knew that I would never change my mind—and I also knew that for someone just out of high school I was doing pretty well. I had my job writing the "Hospital News" for Hampton Hospital, and at night I worked on *All the Slow Dances*.

Then, after months of silence, the letters began coming. From Zurich, Switzerland.

3

LET ME MAKE this clear to you. Arnold and I had been out of touch with each other for ten months. I had asked him to marry me, he had refused. I had asked him to come back to the States with me, and he had refused that too. So I had not written him—though there was not a day of my life, not an hour of it, when he was out of my mind. As far as I was concerned, Arnold and I were already married in some strange and psychic way. However. Begging was something I could not do—because fat as I was,

17

and short as I was, and insecure as I was, I did have my pride. So I had not written Arnold a single letter in all those months. And then his letters began. And all of them beautiful.

> I sit by the window of my little room [one of the letters said] and wait for dawn to come up over Lake Zurich. I hear the cry of the gulls and the first church bells of the day—and I think of you. Of the brightness of your eyes, and your lovely hair, and how you have always felt in my arms—perfect, molded to me, as though we had been sculpted by a god. Your sweet mouth, which I have kissed so often, and your dear, very young hands, fill my mind with memories. My dearest Rita, my love, I miss you, and I think of Yeats' lines: "Leave unchanged the hands that I have kissed. For old sake's sake."

Well, let me tell you. This is not exactly the kind of letter one gets from a college freshman. Nor is it the kind of letter most women *ever* receive. So—all over again—I felt my heart begin to hurt, and my limbs tremble, and all of a sudden I wasn't sleeping at night. What is it when a person who is eighteen knows that she will love one man for the rest of her life? Most teenagers go through love affairs like potato chips, but I knew, into my very bones, that I was going to be one of those women who have but one love. And it didn't matter that he was thirty-four years old and penniless. We were the same person—two sides of a single coin.

In the ten months since I had seen Arnold, I had had only one date—with a kid in my class named Christopher Flynn—and the only reason I went out with him at all was because he was tiny and harmless, a sort of teenage Truman Capote. Christopher had blond hair and glasses, and he stuttered. So I went out with him one night.

First, we had dinner at a coffee shop in East Hampton. Then we went to the movies. Then we went for ice cream. Then we went over to his house and listened to records. And it was probably the most boring evening of my life. I mean, after two years of loving Arnold, I was not exactly turned on by a tiny eighteen-year-old whose one passion in life was old Beatles records. I felt like I was dating a child. And all I could think of that evening was Arnold. His letters. The beauty in them. And the fact that I was not answering.

"I'm just crazy about 'Strawberry Fields Forever,' aren't you?" Christopher was saying.

"Yes," I sighed. "I'm mad about it."

We were sitting together on Christopher's couch. The living room was done entirely in green and made me a little seasick. The walls were green, the rugs were green, and even the lamps gave off a

19

greenish light. Why are your parents so turned on by the color green? I wanted to say—but didn't.

Christopher rose to his feet and put on the flip side of the record. Now we had "Lucy in the Sky with Diamonds." A terrible tune.

Christopher sat down again, a little closer to me this time. "I'm really glad you came out with me this evening, Rita. I had a really good time."

"Me too," I said bleakly.

Christopher edged closer. I couldn't see the expression in his eyes because his eyeglasses were so thick. Oh God, I thought, here it comes. He wants to make out with me. This child, this young boy. "Rita?" said Christopher.

"Yes?" I replied.

"There's something I've wanted to say to you for a long time. For around six months now."

I gave my date a cold look. "So, what is it? Shoot."

Christopher looked embarrassed. "It's this way. Around six months ago I read an article in a magazine that I wanted to share with you. But I'm sort of shy, so I didn't. But I really wanted you to know about it Rita, because I like you."

"So?" I said. "So?"

"It was an article about fat people. Fat women, I mean. And it was all about this ranch out west where fat women can go to get thin. The basis of the treatment is sleep. They give you a shot of some kind and you fall asleep for six months. And you lose weight."

I gazed at Christopher for a long long time. "Well, Christopher," I said, "that's very nice of you. To have thought of me, I mean. The whole thing sounds very restful."

"It is!" he exclaimed. "That's the point. Since you're asleep the whole time, you don't have to worry about diets and counting calories. They make it easy for you."

"Why don't they just murder the women?" I suggested.

"What?"

"Why don't they just kill them? Death is the ultimate diet, after all. Corpses lose weight like crazy."

I could see that I had shocked Christopher, but what the hell. And while I knew that he meant to be kind, and was not out to rape me that evening, and probably just wanted to be pals, the discussion turned me to stone. I mean—cement. So I got out of there fast, telling dear Christopher that I would take the bus home, and thanking him for the wonderful evening—and all the way back to Sag Harbor I did some very hard thinking. Because Christopher Flynn had reacted to me the way that every man in my life had reacted to me since I hit puberty—as a fat girl. None of them saw me as intelligent,

21

or funny, or original, because all they could see was the fat. God! I had even learned recently—from a program on television—that there are social clubs for fat women where they can go to meet men who are turned on by fat. These poor souls get dressed up in low-cut dresses, and jewelry, and high heels, and go to these places where all the men are looking to get laid—not by women, but by fat. "Some men *like* fat," one of the women on the program had explained. "They like the weight of it, the feel of it, the softness of it. I guess it makes them think of their mothers."

The point is, even tiny Christopher Flynn saw me as a fat girl and nothing more. Only Arnold had ever found me beautiful. He had found me beautiful fat, and he had found me beautiful forty pounds thinner—and if I became a blimp, a freak, an anomaly, an aberration, he would find that beautiful too. I had spent my entire life trying to diet, losing weight and gaining it back—and now I was finished. Little Christopher Flynn had done me more of a favor than he knew, because I was finished with the whole goddam thing. I would be who I was—and if that person was a fat person, fine. I would no longer diet and I would no longer count calories and go to weight doctors and join therapy groups. What I would be was MYSELF.

Meanwhile, the letters from Arnold kept coming—one more beautiful than the next—and every letter said that he missed me. What had prompted this outpouring I could not imagine—but I did not write back. Some instinct told me to keep quiet, to bide my time, to wait and see what would happen. And then the same instinct told me that Arnold was about to come home. He may not have known this himself, but he was getting ready to return to America, and Sag Harbor—and me.

Early in June, a cable arrived. "RETURNING JULY 20 KENNEDY AIRPORT SWISSAIR FLIGHT 100 WILL YOU MEET ME QUESTIONMARK ARNOLD."

I read the cable twice and sank down in my father's lounge chair—all the breath knocked out of me. And I didn't know whether to laugh or cry, so I did a bit of both. Thank God I had written that letter to Hofstra University! Because now, more than ever, I was sure of my path. Arnold and I would get married and both of us would write. We would put an end to all these months of indecision and start our life together.

It took me five days to work up the courage to speak to my parents, and then, when I did, there was an explosion as big as an H bomb. Not only did I explain that I was not going to college in the fall, I also explained that Arnold Bromberg was

23

coming back. Poor Mom. Poor Daddy. They had thought that Arnold was a thing of the past, a dead issue, and now I was talking about him again.

"I went to Switzerland to see him," I said, "last August. I stayed five days. I told you I was visiting Corry Brown in New York City, but it was a lie. I'm sorry."

All this was taking place at the dinner table—which, for us, means the small round table in the kitchen. My father had had his usual number of beers, and his face was flushed. My mother's face was dead white. "I don't know what you're telling us, Rita," she said. "It's like a dream, a bad dream."

"I'm sorry, Mom. But I'm still in love with Arnold, and from his letters I know that he's still in love with me. It never ended, you see. Our relationship."

"But to lie to us, about so many things . . ."

"I had to lie! You forced me to lie, both of you. Don't you think I would rather have told the truth? But you and Daddy have always been hostile to Arnold."

"Hostile?" yelled my father. "This bum, this loser, is about to wreck your life, and we're supposed to stand by and let it happen? *No way.* Your mother and I did not raise you to marry a freak."

"Oh Daddy," I sighed. "You're so blind to anyone different from yourself. Arnold is a genius."

"Rita," my mother said in a strangled voice, "we can't let this happen to you. What kind of parents would we be if we didn't try to protect you?"

And that's when I lost my cool. "Protect me! Christ, Mother, I'm eighteen years old! How much longer can you go on protecting me? Until I'm forty? This is my *life* we're talking about. And I have a right to do with it what I want."

My mother gave me a hard look. "I hope you have a child of your own someday. Then you'll understand what's taking place here. You'll look back and you'll understand."

I was out of control now, and I knew it. "To hell with both of you!" I cried.

My father rose to his feet, pushing back his chair. "You get involved with that joker again, and I'll have him arrested."

"On what grounds? I'm eighteen now, Daddy, I'm of age!"

"OK," he said. "You're so grown up, go out and earn some money and contribute to this household. And I don't mean by writing the hospital news."

"That's not fair."

"So when was life ever fair!" he shouted. "You have a lot to learn, kiddo, a great deal!"

And then he stormed out of the house.

My mother came over to where I was sitting and put her hand on my shoulder. "Sweetie," she said tentatively, "I know that you think you love this man—and I know that it's been going on for two years. But you haven't had enough experience yet to know *what* you want. Don't throw your life away."

"How old were you when you married Daddy?" I asked.

"Nineteen."

"And did you have a lot of experience?"

"No, I didn't. I was just a young girl in love. Like you. But I should have waited."

"And *not* married Daddy?"

"I didn't say that. But I should have had more experience of the world before I married—not just given in to romance."

I tried to think of my father being romantic, and couldn't. "You have to let me live my own life," I said to her.

My mother gave me a sad smile. "That's what I used to say to my mother, too. Isn't it awful how things repeat themselves?"

My mother did something unexpected. She put her cheek against my head and kissed my hair. "I wish I could spare you," she said. "I wish I could spare you the whole darn thing."

4

ON THE AFTERNOON of July 20th, I sat in a glass-enclosed visitors' lounge in Kennedy airport. Arnold's plane was due at three o'clock, and it was already three fifteen. I had been to the ladies' room four times, to look at myself, and while I wasn't satisfied with what I saw in the mirror, there wasn't much I could do about it. I had made a decision that morning to meet Arnold at the airport as *me*—and me meant blue jeans and a pink shirt, and a pink ribbon in my hair. That is the way he had left me, and that is the way he would find me. Rita Formica, short, fat, but honest.

Even though the lounge was air conditioned, I was sweating under my shirt—and because I had recently stopped smoking, I felt jittery. I popped some Tic-Tac mints in my mouth and looked at my watch again. The plane was twenty minutes late.

And then the screen showed that Flight 100, from Zurich, had just landed.

I am not a person given to prayers, but I did start to pray at that moment. And what I asked God for was control. I asked him to not let me burst into tears at the first sight of Arnold, or make a fool of myself in any way.

It seemed to take hours, but eventually the passengers from Flight 100 got through customs and began to appear, carrying their luggage. Oh God, I thought, where is he? Oh God, please let everything go well. Don't let me fall apart. Give me control.

I didn't recognize Arnold at first—he seemed so much taller, so much larger than I remembered. But yes, there he was, wearing a dark summer suit and a dark tie. He was also wearing sunglasses and had a briefcase under one arm. He could have been a movie star. A large rumpled one, like the young Orson Welles.

"Arnold!" I called. "Over here!"

He saw me, and his face broke into a smile. He took off the dark glasses and waved at me. "Rita!" he cried.

It was strange, but we did not embrace. We just stood there looking at each other, and I couldn't believe how wonderful he looked. Large, tan, his brown hair very bushy, his bright eyes very green. He was not wearing sneakers, but some very interesting European shoes. His suitcase was new.

"Hello there, darling," said Arnold. He was looking at me in a way that was almost bemused, smiling, shaking his head.

"Hi," I said. "You look different."

28

"How?" he asked.

I grinned. "European, sort of. *Zurichoise.*"

"Have you got a kiss for an old friend?" he asked.

Tears came into my eyes, but I stopped them at the source. "Sure," I said. "Be my guest."

He put down his things, and took my face between his hands, and kissed me. Gently. Softly. The kiss I had been waiting for for ten months. "It's been a long time," he said.

I could not speak, and so I simply nodded—too overwhelmed to trust myself with words. My feelings had not lied to me. For ten long months my feelings had been right. I loved this man and would never love anyone else.

"Was the flight OK?" I asked.

He was gazing at me, drinking me in. "Yes, perfect. I sat next to a psychologist. An interesting man."

"Is that your only suitcase?"

"Yes. Just the one."

How typical, I thought, that Arnold should have only one suitcase. He had been abroad for over a year and had accumulated nothing. "What's in the briefcase?" I asked him.

"My manuscript, darling. My book."

"Did you finish it?"

"Not yet. Not quite yet."

We went outside—into the steamy weather—and looked for the Hamptons bus. "I got you a room at the Harborside Motel," I said to Arnold. "Not too expensive."

He smiled at me. "Does it have a double bed?"

"What do you think?"

As the bus pulled away from the airport, Arnold leaned back in his seat and took my hand. "I can't tell you how wonderful you look."

"I'm still fat," I said.

"And still beautiful," he replied.

I lifted his hand to my lips and kissed it. Then I leaned back and shut my eyes. The bus was working its way toward the Long Island Expressway. In two hours we would be in Sag Harbor. "Why did you come back?" I asked Arnold. "It surprised me."

He turned and looked at me, his eyes probing mine. "You never answered my letters."

"So?"

"So I got frightened. I thought perhaps it was over."

"You could have phoned me, Arnold."

"I didn't want to get your parents on the phone."

"Ah, I see."

We were on the expressway now and the bus had picked up some speed. "Why didn't you write me?" he asked.

"I don't know. It seemed better not to."

30

"Your silence hurt me."

Hurt? I thought. Oh, Arnold dear, you don't know the meaning of the word.

"Never mind," I said. "We're together again now. How's the organ playing? How's your teacher at the Fraumunster?"

"Herr Kubli retired a few months ago. I miss him terribly."

"Is that why you came home? Because Herr Kubli retired?"

Arnold gazed at me. "No, Rita. I came home to be with you. To marry you."

For one long moment, my heart stopped. I mean, stopped in its tracks. By the time it started beating again, I had regained my cool. "Let's talk about that later," I said.

Arnold's motel room was small but very nice—with a view of the harbor. The window looked out at a marina. In the distance was the North Haven bridge. "How lovely it is here!" Arnold said, standing by the window. "I'd forgotten."

"Still the same old town. Jammed with tourists in summer, and lonely in winter."

"That's what I like about it."

I was sitting on the edge of the bed, studying the room. There was a kitchenette off the bathroom. "I'll bring you some things to make coffee with," I said. "And some staples."

31

Arnold came over to me. "Have you told your parents I'm here?"

"Yes. I also told them I would be staying with you tonight."

A look of surprise crossed his face, but he didn't say anything. And for a moment, my mind raced back to the scene that had taken place two days ago. In plain and simple language, I had told my parents that I would be staying at the Harborside Motel with Arnold on his first night home. And, let me tell you, had I just announced that I had murdered the Pope, it couldn't have been worse. My mother went pale as death, and my father—after his first outburst—started to cry. You would have thought that I was off to prison for the rest of my life, not just off to make love. And this is the part that amazed me, and continues to amaze me. The fact that my sex life disturbed them so much. I mean, didn't *they* have a sex life? And hadn't they had one since their teens? Why couldn't I have a sex life too? I was not an amoeba, given to asexual reproduction. I was a woman.

Arnold took off his jacket. Then he went into the bathroom and washed his face. "I've got jet lag," he said. "I feel tired."

"So come to bed, Arnold. Come and rest."

He walked over and sat down next to me, on the bed. "I love you so much," he said—and the words

32

were my undoing. I mean, he sounded so young as he said them, like a boy. I looked at this large tousled man, with his beautiful eyes and distinguished face, and felt a stab of pain in my heart. "I love you too," I said. "Very much."

He kissed me and the kiss was gentle—but underneath it was a hurricane, a volcano. I didn't have to ask him if he'd been faithful to me, because his hunger was all too apparent. And the thing that surprised me was that his hunger meant more to me than my own. This very sensual man had been faithful to me for ten months, and I knew what that meant. And so I began to make love to him with all the skill that I had—the skill he had taught me long ago.

We took off our clothes and lay down together, feeling waves of love wash over us like waves from the sea. His mouth tasted salty, and his body was so beautiful, so strong, that I caught my breath as I caressed it. How beautiful you are! I said to him, and he laughed and said that men are not beautiful. But they are, I murmured. More beautiful than women, really, and you are the most beautiful of them all.

And then the months that we had been apart were washed away—by that invisible sea—and we were together again, molded and sculpted by some ancient god. His body and my body. Together.

33

5

I WOKE AT DAWN to hear sea gulls screaming in the harbor. The day was already hot, but a breeze moved the curtains at the window. Arnold slept deeply, his head on my breast, a little smile on his face. What a miracle we are together, I thought. And then reality began to impinge. My parents, a place for Arnold to live, money. There was going to be a lot to cope with, and I wondered if I had the strength to do it. Yes, I told myself. I did.

Arnold stirred and pulled me close to him. "What time is it?" he asked.

"Five thirty."

"It seems much later."

I kissed him. "Your sense of time is off. Jet lag."

"I'm hungry," he said, opening his eyes.

"For breakfast?" I inquired. "I can go out and get some."

"Not for breakfast. Hungry for you."

And so we made love again, as the gulls in the harbor screamed and the sounds of traffic began on the North Haven bridge. Then I took a shower and went out to a coffee shop for our breakfast. By nine that morning we were sitting by the window having coffee and cold croissants. A carton of orange juice. Some slices of ham. "It's so strange to be back here," said Arnold. "So wonderful."

"Do you think you'll miss Zurich?" I asked.

He took a swallow of coffee. "I don't know, darling. But I would like us to go back someday. It's such an exciting city, so small and yet so cosmopolitan. The theater there is wonderful, by the way. I started going to the *Schauspielhaus*. They've been having an Ibsen festival."

Arnold had surprised me, the few days I had spent with him in Zurich, because he had spoken German, and paid for things, and read the local papers like a native. When I first met him, he had had all the sophistication of a small-town minister. But in Zurich he had acquired a certain flair. He still had that flair, but the funny thing was, I felt that I now had some too.

"Do you mind if I smoke?" Arnold asked, taking a package of cigarets from his briefcase.

"Of course not, Arnold. But I wish you had stopped."

"I'll stop soon. For your sake."

I looked quickly at him, because there was something new in his voice, something that I didn't understand. "What are you thinking?" I asked.

"About us. About getting married."

As though my mind were a film that had speeded up, I suddenly saw our entire affair. It was playing in my mind like a movie, and the events of the story were clear as glass. It was not a very complicated story, after all, simply the story of a young girl who falls in love with an older man. The girl is fat, but determined. The man is a kind of poet, beautiful and impractical. The parents disapprove, so the lovers part. But this parting makes them more in love than ever. They meet briefly in a European city. They make love. They part again, and then, ten months later, the man becomes terribly lonely, returns to America, and asks the girl—at last—to marry him.

The important part of the story is this. The man is asking the girl to marry him out of *need*. Out of hunger. Out of loneliness.

"Arnold," I said slowly, "I don't think we should get married. I think we should live together first."

As I mentioned to you before, Arnold had a tan—acquired, perhaps, in some Alpine village during a holiday. But now, beneath the tan, he went pale. "I don't understand you, Rita."

"I think we should know each other better. Before we get married, I mean."

"*Know* each other better?"

I pulled my chair close to his. "Arnold dearest, we don't really know each other at all. We just like to make love a lot, and that isn't a basis for marriage. I mean, it seems like a basis, but I don't think it is. Let's rent an apartment somewhere and try the whole thing out."

Arnold frowned and blew a smoke ring into the air. "You amaze me," he said.

"Why?"

"Because you have told me a hundred times that you wanted to get married. And now, when at last I am ready . . ."

"But that's the point, Arnold. You're *not* ready. And neither am I. Let's live together first."

"But your parents will . . ."

I gave him a determined look. "Leave them to me. They're my problem and I'll cope with it."

Arnold went over to the bed, where he stretched out. "You certainly have changed, my darling. I don't know what to make of it."

I smiled at him. "Frankly, Arnold, I don't know what to make of it myself."

MY PARENTS WERE waiting for me when I came home that afternoon, sitting at the kitchen table as though they were at a wake. My wake. I had an image of my body lying in the next room, surrounded by candles. It looked terrible.

"Hi," I said with false cheeriness. "I'm home."

Nobody said anything. They just stared at me.

I went over to the refrigerator and took out a

37

carton of juice. "Hot day," I said. "Really humid."

They still didn't say anything, so I poured myself some juice and sat down at the kitchen table. "So?" I said. "What's happened? Have the Russians landed, or what?"

"Where have you been since yesterday?" my father asked.

"At the Harborside Motel. With Arnold. We had a lot to work out."

"I'll bet you did," said my father. "I'll just bet you did."

"Tony . . ." my mother began.

"Keep out of this!" he snapped. "I'll handle it! Rita, I want you to listen to me carefully. We do not want you to see this Bromberg fellow again. And if you do see him again, then I'm filing charges against him. And don't ask me what kind of charges, because I'll find some! Your mother and I do not want you involved with this person."

"Tell me why," I said.

"Why?" my father roared. "OK, we'll tell you why. Because this joker is twice as old as you are and doesn't have two nickels to rub together. Because he's never had a profession. Because he's a loser, Rita, a goddam loser. He comes to Sag Harbor from out west somewhere, and opens a string of asshole businesses, cheesecake, you name it, and he goes bust. Then he seduces my kid, and then he

takes off for Europe. What would you call this? Responsible behavior?"

"Daddy!" I said. "You're twisting the whole thing so horribly that it's unrecognizable. You're slanting it."

"Tony," said my mother, "you *are* slanting the facts. Mr. Bromberg is a writer and he's halfway through some kind of book. He's very well educated, too. And he plays the organ."

"Great!" yelled my father. "I'll get them an organ for a wedding present!"

"We're not getting married," I said quietly. "Not yet. We've decided to live together first."

My father's face twitched. "What are you talking about?"

"We've decided to live together for a while. So we can get to know each other."

My mother was turning her head back and forth between the two of us as though she were at a tennis match. I was touched that she had stuck up for me, but I knew it wouldn't do any good.

"If you set up housekeeping with this loser, then you're not welcome here anymore," said my father. "You don't ask me for money, and you don't come back when it's over."

I hadn't meant to cry, but I was crying all the same—crying at the goddam unfairness of the situation, and crying because I felt so alone.

"Daddy," I said, "if Arnold's a loser, then I'm one too. Because we're very much alike. We love the same things, and we have the same ideals, and we both want to be writers and everything."

"Writers! And what will you write? How will you pay the bills? Because I assure you, kiddo, that I'm not putting out a penny."

"It isn't money I want from you," I said. "It's understanding."

And then I walked out.

I was still crying as I walked down Madison Street, and because I didn't know where to go, I headed for the Heavenly Cafe, my old stamping grounds, the place where I had gone since childhood to assuage my sorrows. The Heavenly Cafe has booths with cracked leather seats, and terrible pictures on the walls, and scuffed tiles on the floor, but it has always been my second home.

I went in, sat down at the counter, and ordered an extra-thick coffee malted. It was not what I had planned on ordering, but, as usual, I needed to soothe myself with food. And as I sipped the malted, my mind skimmed over the eighteen years of my life like a dragonfly. I saw myself at the age of five, stealing food from the neighbors because I was always so hungry. I saw myself at eight, being taken to a diet doctor in New York City. Then I saw myself at ten, being sent to a camp in the Poconos for fat children. The place was called Camp Willow, and the food the children were given was so limited that some of the kids would eat toothpaste. Yes, toothpaste. Here's how a typical therapy session would go—the characters being a lot of little fat girls and the camp director, Miss Geary.

FRANCIE: Miss Geary, Marsha is eating toothpaste again.
MARSHA: I'm not! That's a lie!
MISS GEARY: Are you eating toothpaste, Marsha?
MARSHA: No.
MISS GEARY: What kind of toothpaste are you eating, dear?
MARSHA (*starting to cry*):   I am not eating any toothpaste.
MISS GEARY (*kindly*):   There's nothing wrong with eating toothpaste, Marsha. You're a fat person, and fat people do peculiar things. That's why we're all here. To stop our peculiar behavior. To stop eating toothpaste.

Forgive the digression—because the point is not that so many of us ate toothpaste that summer, the point is that by the time I was twelve my father had spent so much money on me. Diet camps, diet doctors, psychotherapists, hypnosis, and now . . . and now his investment was going bust. This in-

Conejos County Library
La Jara, Colorado 81140

41

credible investment named Rita Formica was not paying dividends, and so he was furious. It wasn't that Arnold was a penniless writer, and it wasn't even that Arnold seemed like an oddball. It was the fact that my father had invested his whole life in me, and now the investment was slipping away.

When I got back to the motel, Arnold was in bed, smoking a cigaret and reading a book. "Hi, darling," he said cheerfully. "How did it go?"

"Well . . ." I said, "it was rough. I'll tell you another time."

I sat down on the bed. "What are you reading?" I asked.

"It's called *The Unexpected Universe*. By a man named Stallings. Part philosophy, part physics."

"Well. That's nice."

I went into the kitchenette, to put away the groceries I had bought. Coffee, milk, some sweet rolls, some cheese, two apples. "Arnold?" I said.

"Hmm?" he replied.

I walked back to the bed. "Could I ask you something?"

"Of course, darling. Sit down."

I could tell that his mind was still on the book, but I needed to talk to him. "Arnold—what are your plans? For the future, I mean."

He gazed at me lovingly. "Plans, dearest?"

"Well yes, plans. I mean, what do you want to do with the next few years? Do you know?"

"Of course I know," he said gently. "I want to live with you, and work on my book. I want to take long walks on the beach."

"Is that all?"

"Of course not. I also want to keep up with my organ studies. I made such progress last year with Herr Kubli."

"Well then," I said tentatively, "what do we do for funds? You know. Money."

He frowned. "I don't really know."

"You mean you haven't thought about it?"

"Actually, I haven't," he said. "Look darling, don't worry about it. We'll work something out."

He smiled at me and went back to reading his book. But a chill had gone down my spine, to the very bottom of it, and there it remained—like a lump of ice. I lay down next to him as he continued to read, but my mind was spinning. For the next year, said my inner voice, Arnold intends to write, and play the organ, and take walks on the beach. Does he think you are an heiress? Gloria Vanderbilt? Christina Onassis? Who's going to buy the groceries and who will pay the rent? Suppose you get pregnant? You won't, you won't, said a second voice, you're on the Pill. But how are you going

43

to *manage* all this? asked the first voice. Your father has kicked you out.

What are bridges for, asked the second voice—except to be burned.

7

THE NEXT MORNING, as Arnold continued to read about the universe, I went out to find us a place to live. We had made love until three in the morning, and I was tired. Physically tired, and mentally tired as well. Because it was beginning to occur to me that our situation was not as simple as it had first seemed. Arnold, who had been living in Zurich on an advance from a New York publisher, had told me last night that he was down to six hundred dollars. I myself had four hundred in my savings account, and that was all.

I bought the local paper, went into the Heavenly Cafe for coffee, and turned to the real estate section. Under "For Rent, Year-round," there were no apartments at all, just houses. And some of them cost one thousand dollars a month. So what did you expect? I asked myself. This is the Hamptons. The rents are high.

I continued to peruse the real estate page. "Beach cottage with Jacuzzi, library, and three bedrooms,"

I read. "Fully furnished. September to April, $15,000.00."

I kept on reading. And there, suddenly, was an ad for a house we could afford. The ad was in a box all by itself and said *Handyman Special. North Haven.*

> For rent. Large one-room house near Shelter Island Ferry. Wood stove, fantastic wrap-around views. Needs work, but will give two-year lease. $250.00 a month.

I raced over to the pay phone at the end of the restaurant and phoned the number given. A woman answered, who agreed to meet me at the house in one hour. "You can't miss it," she said. "It's the last house on Route 114 before the ferry."

I hurried back to the motel, where Arnold was still reading, and told him the news. "It's only two hundred and fifty a month!" I said. "And if they don't want a security deposit, I think we can do it."

The Shelter Island ferry is three miles from Sag Harbor, so we had to take a taxi. We arrived at the house on time, but my heart sank when I saw it, because "handyman special" was putting it mildly. The place was a wreck. I mean, the roof was sagging in, and the paint was peeling, and the garden

45

had grown up around the house like a jungle. Arnold, however, didn't notice any of this "Look at the view!" he exclaimed. "It's sublime."

Well yes, I suppose it was. Because the house was on a little cliff, and everywhere you looked there was water. Across the channel, Shelter Island glowed in the sunlight. The ferryboat was crossing back and forth. Sea gulls wheeled and cried. "I'm *mad* about this place," said Arnold.

Mrs. Cameron, the owner, was a few minutes late—but when she did arrive, she took us through the house as if it were a mansion. "You see?" she kept saying brightly, "the place is *very* well equipped. All the kitchen appliances work. And so does the bathroom."

I walked around the house feeling dubious. Because while there was indeed a kitchen at the end of the one large room, its appliances were pretty old. And the "bathroom" was just an enclosed toilet. "Where does one take a bath?" I asked Mrs. Cameron. Without blinking an eye, she said, "Why, in summer, you can walk right down to the beach! Just a few steps away."

And in winter? I wanted to ask. But something told me that Arnold and I would never find such a low rent again, and so I asked Mrs. Cameron if she wanted a security deposit. "No, no," she said sweetly. "I can tell that you're a young married

46

couple, just starting out. We don't need any deposit."

So right there, on the spot, we signed a two-year lease. Arnold seemed to have no compunction in signing the document, but I felt very nervous. I had signed my name as Rita Bromberg.

"What do we do about heat?" I asked Mrs. Cameron. "In winter, I mean."

Mrs. Cameron's cheerfulness seemed to be wearing thin. "You use the wood stove," she said. "It's perfectly adequate."

"Oh, I'm sure it is," Arnold replied. "I'm sure everything will be fine."

Handing us the keys, and our copy of the lease, Mrs. Cameron took off like a shot. Our rent, she had explained, would not start until September. Until then, we could do some work on the place.

"Arnold," I said thoughtfully, "are you handy in any way? I mean with plumbing or carpentry?"

But Arnold was already heading down to the beach—our beach—from which you could see Shelter Island, and far in the distance, the North Fork of Long Island. "This is wonderful!" he cried.

I joined him on the beach, and holding hands we began to stroll along at the water's ege. Even though the day was hot, a strong wind was coming off the Sound. A flock of cormorants flew over our heads.

" 'I will arise and go now—and go to Innisfree!' " Arnold shouted into the wind. " 'And a small cabin build there, of clay and wattles made.' "

"Ezra Pound!" I shouted to him.

"Wrong!" he shouted back. "Yeats!"

And we collapsed on the sand with laughter.

The following day, when my parents were out, I removed all of my clothes from their home—and dragged the suitcases over to the Harborside Motel. Arnold had snapped into action too, and had phoned the local storage company to deliver his books to the Ferry House, as we called it. Owning not a stick of furniture, Arnold did have books. Hundreds of them.

I was stumped about what to do for furniture, but only momentarily. Phoning my old mentor, Doris Morris, I asked if there was anything in her attic that she could loan us. The ex-chorus girl, turned writer, turned agent, said that of course there was. Beds, bureaus, anything. All of which gave me some guilt—because I owed her a lot of money for that trip to Zurich. I *will* pay you back someday, I said in my mind. The minute things improve.

My parents had given me a Honda motorbike for my eighteenth birthday, and when this vehicle was liberated from the garage, it made my life easier. Traveling back and forth on the Honda, I moved all of my clothes. Then the moving and storage company delivered Arnold's books. Miss Morris sent the furniture over in a van.

Sheets and towels from the dime store. Two warm blankets from Caldor's. Pots and pans from the thrift shop, and some dishes too. Unashamed, I rescued an old rug someone on Madison Street had tossed into the garbage, and had it dry cleaned. Using bricks and boards, Arnold constructed bookshelves.

On September 1st, we moved into the Ferry House. It was still a wreck, but at least the place was clean. A fanatic about cleanliness, Arnold had scrubbed the house from top to bottom, especially the stove and refrigerator. There was exactly one closet for all of our clothes. Between us, we had one bureau. No TV, no radio, and a very scanty supply of hot water from an ancient hot water heater. Nevertheless. It was our home and we were thrilled.

That first evening at the Ferry House, Arnold cooked us a beautiful meal—fresh bluefish and a salad, with cherry tarts for dessert—and then we went out to the porch and looked at the night. The midnight-blue sky was trembling with stars, and somewhere in the woods an owl was hooting. The little ferry passed us, on its constant journey, its port and starboard lights shining. "How beautiful this is," said Arnold. "How lucky we are."

That night, as we made love, I knew that he was right. We were lucky—to have each other, and to have our own little house, and to be able to look toward the future together. The only trouble was . . . we were running out of cash.

IF YOU ARE THINKING that I had been out of touch with my parents during these weeks, you're dead wrong. Because for some reason I had a strange desire to phone my mother every day—the same desire I used to have at summer camp. So, at exactly ten o'clock each morning, when I knew my father would be at the auto shop, I phoned Mom and told her what was going on with Arnold and me. "You'll have to come over soon," I told her. "We're really fixing the place up."

"Your father is suffering," my mother said during one of these conversations. "Drop him a little note or something."

"No way," I replied. "But I would like *you* to come over very soon. You haven't seen Arnold for a year and a half. And he's your prospective son-in-law."

"Has he got a job yet?"

"Mother," I said in a steely voice, "you know that Arnold's writing a book. That's his job."

Privately, however, I was worried. Because Arnold and I were going through our money like it was Kleenex. We had had a phone installed, which cost money, and had had the roof partially repaired—which also cost money—and pretty soon we would have to buy cords of wood for the wood stove.

I don't know how Arnold and I, together, both tacitly assumed that it would be me who would go out and get a job to support us, but that was the assumption. Arnold, after all, was working on his book every morning—on a secondhand typewriter which had cost, yes, money—and spent the rest of the day cooking, taking long walks, and reading poetry on the beach. His library, which he had brought to Sag Harbor from Kansas two years ago, was really very impressive and contained a lot of rare books and first editions.

So once again I traveled to town to get the local paper and read the classified pages. The "Help Wanted" ads were not as numerous as they had been in the spring, and also, some of the ads were a little weird. "Shepherd wanted to tend small flock of sheep in Bridgehampton," said one ad. "Soprano needed for weddings and funerals," said another.

"Energetic people wanted for Sag Harbor dog

51

census," said a more interesting ad. "Ten dollars an hour."

That one sounded feasible, so I raced to the phone and called the number given. Applicants, said the man I spoke to, were supposed to come over to the town hall and see the dog warden.

To make a long story short, by that afternoon I had become a census taker. The reason for the whole thing was that the Suffolk County Department of Health was doing a dog census of the Hamptons— this area having a huge, and perhaps unhealthy, number of dogs. It was a strange job, but what the hell. I had my Honda, to get me back and forth to town.

However. There are certain jobs that lose their charm very quickly, and this was one of them. There were four of us taking the census, each with his own section of town to cover, and my section, of course, was the seedy part—over near Lawrence Street. The first house I approached was not a house but a Quonset hut, and the man who opened the door smelled of booze. "I'm from the Department of Health," I explained, "and I'd like to ask if you have a dog." "A dog?" the man said. "Yeah, my wife." And he slammed the door.

From house to house. In sunny weather and rainy weather, five hours a day, carrying my Department of Health census sheets and trying to seem official.

Some people were never home, and some others who were home were incredibly rude. Certain people would not let me in, while others wanted to *give* me their dog. "You want him?" one man said. "He's a very nice dog, very gentle." Then there were days when the dogs in question tried to attack me—and days when various housewives would tell me how to lose weight. I mean, one of the burdens of being fat is that everyone feels he or she has a right to comment on it. A year ago, a woman walking down Main Street, a perfect stranger, had stopped me and said, "Honey, I have this fabulous doctor . . ." and now various local housewives were doing the same. After revealing to me whether or not they had a dog—and what breed it was—they would invite me inside to have coffee and to tell me about the diet that had changed their lives. Lettuce diets, rice diets, fruit diets, liquid protein diets, et al.

I had always had the fantasy that if I lost weight, my problems would disappear. But then I lost weight and lost Arnold at the same time—to Switzerland— so I began to realize that the idea was an illusion. The concept that thin equals no problems and no rejections is crazy.

Anyway. From eight to one every day I did my census taking, and then I would ride my Honda over to the hospital, to gather information for

"Hospital News." From floor to floor I traveled, getting the latest info from nurses and doctors, secretaries and technicians. The hospital now had a CAT scanner, I was told. The gift shop would soon be remodeled.

By midafternoon I would be back in Sag Harbor, to shop for groceries and pick up our laundry at the Laundromat. And then, the little Honda buzzing away, I would head for the Ferry House—to do domestic chores for the rest of the afternoon and work on "Hospital News" at night. At sunset, Arnold and I would go down to the beach to watch the spectacle of a flaming red sun disappear over the North Fork. Then Arnold would cook dinner.

It wasn't a bad life, but there was one thing about it that gave me grief. My book, *All the Slow Dances*, was gathering dust in a bureau drawer. Sometimes, when Arnold was sleeping, I would take it out and read the first few chapters, surprised at how good it was, and then I would slip it back into the bureau. Arnold's book was more important than mine just now, I told myself. My own book would have to wait.

Another thing that got to me was that all my friends had gone off to college. I mean, I had thought that this wouldn't bother me in the least, but it did. Corry Brown, my friend in New York City, had departed for Vassar, and even tiny Christopher

Flynn—optimistic as always—was ensconced at Middlebury. I tried to picture myself as a college freshman, carrying my books across some green and grassy campus, and couldn't. I tried to picture myself sitting in an English class, sipping a malted at the campus coffee shop, going to a prom. No way, no way. For better or worse, I had gone beyond that now.

9

TOWARD THE END OF September, my mother announced that she was coming over for tea. I had invited her a dozen times, she had refused, but now, she said, she was ready to appear. Nervous as hell, Arnold and I cleaned the house from top to bottom, bought two new chairs, purchased some teacups at the thrift shop, and went out to the woods—where we cut pine boughs to arrange in a bowl. Domestic as always, Arnold decided to bake some oatmeal cookies for the event. I washed my hair—in the kitchen sink—and set it.

The day was cloudy and cool, and just before Mom was due to appear, I sent up a little prayer to God, asking that he let the sun shine. I wanted everything to look as nice as possible—and more than anything, I wanted Mom to like Arnold. She had met him before, of course, but had always found him odd.

At exactly four o'clock, my mother's Toyota pulled into our dirt driveway—and from the window, I watched her get out of the car and survey the house. She shook her head a little, then squared her shoulders and came toward the porch. Excited by her arrival, Arnold rushed to the front door, to greet her.

The trouble was this. Arnold had just finished baking his oatmeal cookies and was still wearing an apron. A frilly one, with flowers on it.

"Mrs. Formica!" said Arnold. "How lovely to see you! How nice of you to come!"

My mother looked at Arnold's apron and gave a weak smile. "Hello there, Mr. Bromberg," she said. And to me, she said, "Hi, darling."

"Will you excuse me?" said Arnold. "I was just taking something out of the oven." He hurried back to the stove.

My mother looked at our one-room house. At the shabby furniture, and the peeling paint on the walls, at the big double bed and the little bureau. She looked at the rows and rows of books, and at the old, faded rug. "Well," she said.

"Sit down," I said nervously. "Arnold will bring us some tea."

Gingerly, as though she were sitting on fresh paint, my mother sat down on one of the new wooden chairs. "Do you have heat here?" she asked.

"Oh, yes," I said, "absolutely. Very very good heat. A wood stove."

She glanced across the room, to where the pot-bellied stove sat on its brick pedestal. "You mean that's all you have? A wood stove?"

"Right. And it's very good. I mean, we've only used it a few times, but the heat it gives off is terrific."

Still wearing his apron, Arnold hurried over with the tea tray, on which he had arranged plates, cups, saucers, lemon, sugar, and milk. He placed the tray on our beat-up coffee table and then brought over the teapot and the cookies. He took off his apron. "I'll go down to the beach and bring up some drift-wood for the fire," he said. "You ladies can talk together."

Whistling cheerfully, he departed. The minute he was gone, my mother looked at me. "Oh, sweetie," she said, "this is terrible."

"What's terrible?" I asked brightly, pouring out the tea, and putting some cookies on her plate.

"*This,*" she said, gesturing around the room.

"It's only temporary, Mom. And Arnold loves it. He thinks it has atmosphere."

"But darling, you need so many things."

"Like what?" I asked, pouring myself a cup of the dark Ceylon tea.

"Like everything!" she exclaimed. "I'll have to bring you some things from home."

A pause here to explain that I, Rita Formica—like so many other American kids—had grown up in a house filled with gadgets and appliances. From the time I was born, our house had been crowded with TV sets, and microwave ovens, and leather lounge chairs that gave you a massage. My father had a stationary bicycle and a rowing machine. My mother had her own professional hair drier. We had a food processor and an iron that turned itself off if you forgot it was on. To say nothing of our power mower, for summer—and snow blower, for winter.

All of which, at this particular moment, made me think of Ronnie Gerard, a kid in my class, who during our senior year had worn a T-shirt that said, "At the time of death, the person with the most things, wins."

"I don't need anything," I said to my mother. "We've got all the stuff we need."

My mother put down her tea cup. "Oh sweetie, I wish I understood all this. Why are you living with this man? Is it . . . is it the physical part, or what?"

58

I sighed. The only time that my mother ever mentioned sex to me, it was through a euphemism. "The physical part of marriage," she would say. Or, "*That* part of marriage—you know." It seemed very weird to me that she, a married lady, couldn't come right out and ask me if I liked sleeping with Arnold—but she couldn't. Her nature just wouldn't permit it.

"Arnold and I have a very beautiful sex life," I said, "but that isn't the reason I'm here. I *love* him, Mother, and he loves me. We're happy."

"If your father saw this place, he'd faint."

"Well, that's just too bad!" I replied. "Just too goddam bad."

My mother gave me a sharp look. "Don't swear at me, Rita."

I gave her a sharp look back. "I wasn't."

His arms filled with driftwood, Arnold bustled into the house. "It's *chilly* out there," he said happily. "I'll make us a little fire."

A few minutes later, the three of us were sitting in a circle—Arnold drinking his tea, my mother sitting motionless. Arnold was the only one talking.

"You must come down one evening to watch the sunset with us," he said to my mother. "It's absolutely magnificent from here. In fact, I've been thinking of getting a camera so I can capture it."

An angry look crossed my mother's face. "You

seem to have a great many hobbies, Mr. Bromberg."

"I do, I do," Arnold replied. "Music, poetry, cooking. But photography interests me as well."

"When will your book be finished? Rita tells me that you have a publisher now."

"I do indeed. But I can't really say when it will be done. Writing is so very mysterious—one good day, one bad."

Oh God, I said to myself. Any minute now she will be asking him how he intends to support me and how much money he has in the bank. Isn't it crazy? A man is judged by his money, a woman is judged by her looks.

"Mr. Bromberg . . ." my mother began.

"Yes?" said Arnold.

My mother cleared her throat. "Mr. Bromberg, there are certain things I want to say to you today. And the first is that Rita's father is very upset about this situation."

Arnold seemed genuinely surprised. "Upset? But why?"

"You know all of the reasons," said my mother, "because you heard them in a therapy session almost two years ago. Do you remember?"

"But of course. Mrs. Perlman, the therapist. I remember."

"Well, our feelings haven't changed. I mean, I know you value honesty, Mr. Bromberg, at least that's what you used to say in the past. So I'm being honest. Mr. Formica and I just don't approve."

Arnold gave my mother a long look. "My dear lady," he said gently, "it isn't for you to approve or disapprove. This is Rita's life. She is here of her own free will."

"I know that, I know that," said my mother, "but she is our child, and therefore we're concerned. You don't stop being a parent just because your child comes of age."

"I'm aware of that, dear lady, more aware than you know. Because at thirty-four, *I* am still my mother's little boy. I'd like you to meet my mother, by the way. I think you would find her charming."

"Do you intend to marry Rita?"

"Mother!" I exploded. "For God's sake!"

"It is Rita who doesn't want to get married," Arnold explained. "Not I."

My mother decided to take a new tack. "Mr. Bromberg—Rita's father and I were brought up with certain standards, and we've tried to bring Rita up the same way. She went to Sunday school as a little girl, and she was taught certain things. You can't throw such things out of the window. Morals are morals."

"Morals?" Arnold repeated, as though the word was something new to him. Sanskrit, perhaps, or Chinese.

"Yes, morals! Rita's father and I do not approve of this . . . this domestic arrangement you have. We think it's wrong."

"My dear lady," said Arnold patiently, kindly, "I *cherish* your daughter. Her welfare is my utmost concern. I will love and protect her always."

Well, let me tell you. That one almost did my mother in. Because Arnold's sincerity was beyond question. He meant every word, and the fact that he did—for some reason—upset her. She rose to her feet. "It's obvious that you and I don't speak the same language. I'm sorry, but we don't."

Arnold rose to his feet too. "On the contrary," he said, "we are more in agreement than you know. You want the best for Rita, and so do I. You want her happiness, and I do too. A marriage certificate, a piece of paper, is not the point here. The point is commitment."

And that's when my mother blew her cool. "Commitment! My God, Mr. Bromberg, I don't think you know the meaning of the word! You move here from Kansas and start a cheesecake business. Then you disappear. Then we learn that you've been wandering around Europe. Then you drift back to Sag Harbor—and all this while my little girl has been waiting for you, and mooning over you, and denying her own life. College, a future, security! These are the things she is throwing out the window for you, and I think it's a rotten shame!"

Tears in her eyes, my mother stumbled out the door. "Oh Mom, *please* . . ." I said. But she was already getting into her car.

Arnold went out to the porch and watched the Toyota pull away. He looked very sad. "Never mind," he said, when I joined him. "She'll come around. It's just that you're still her little girl. She cannot think of you as a woman."

"Neither can you," I said under my breath. But what I meant by that, I wasn't really sure.

AS THE DAYS GOT COLDER and the leaves began to turn orange and red, I continued to plug away at my census taking. Then the job was over, which left "Hospital News"—and that obscure publication only paid a hundred dollars a month. I would have to get a new job, and so once again my hours at the Heavenly Cafe were spent scanning the classified ads. Cooks, dental assistants, secretaries. Housekeepers for elderly gentlemen. Carpenters. Nothing, nothing for me at all.

Now that it was autumn, the skies over Shelter Island had become more dramatic. Great banks of clouds, almost low enough to touch, hundreds of migrating geese—and always the little ferry going back and forth. It's funny, but I developed quite a thing about that ferry. I mean, it was so little and tough. Chunky and white, with room for only a few cars, it chugged back and forth across the channel. Some days, the current was so strong that the ferry would have to go sideways, scuttling over to the other side like a crab. Other days, it veered and pitched in the water, breasting the waves. On foggy days, it blew its husky foghorn. On tranquil days, it seemed to glide. Don't ask me why, but I got a crush on the ferryboat that autumn. I would spend whole hours on the beach, watching it.

I got a job for three days putting out a mailing at the local Democratic club. I got a job for ten days painting a woman's guest cottage.

And then something disastrous happened. My Honda was stolen.

Talk about bad luck. I mean, one moment my Honda was sitting outside the Heavenly Cafe, and the next moment it wasn't. I had left the key in the goddam ignition, and the vehicle—my freedom, my wheels—was gone.

I went to the police station and reported the theft—

and then I walked all the way home, to the Ferry House. And for some reason I was crying. It was only a motorbike, but it cost money, dammit, and I didn't know when Arnold and I would be able to afford another. About a mile from home, a woman in a station wagon picked me up and took me the rest of the way. "Is something wrong?" she asked, seeing the tears on my face. "Nothing," I said. "Nothing at all."

I went into the house, but Arnold wasn't there. Then I looked out the front window and saw that he was down on the beach. It was a sunny day, with no wind, and he was reading a book. For one moment, I felt a wild surge of resentment toward him—about everything—and then I went down to the beach. "Arnold!" I said. "Something's happened."

I sat down next to him on the sand and explained about the motorbike. And I was crying all over again, because I had really loved that little machine. It was bright red, with silver accents, and it went fast, used very little gas, and had a good luggage rack. I had liked the way I felt on it too, wearing my helmet and goggles, looking like a chubby Hell's Angel. And now the Honda was gone.

"Now, now," Arnold was saying, as I wept in his arms. "It's not that bad, sweetie. The police will find it. Or we'll get another."

"But we can't get another. They cost a lot of money."

"It'll be all right," said Arnold. "Everything will work out."

"Oh, Arnold," I said, my head buried in his shoulder. "Life is so hard."

"Life," he said patiently, "cannot be characterized."

I pulled away from him, took out a Kleenex, and blew my nose. "You mean, it's *people* who make things easy or hard."

"Exactly. Life itself is neither."

I looked out across the channel. The ferry was gliding toward us, its deck crowded with people. "I wish I knew where we were going," I said. "I wish I knew what lay ahead."

Arnold smiled. "There's an old Zen saying. 'Having no destination, I am never lost.'"

"Huh?"

"Never mind, darling. Things will work out."

"Arnold—how come you never get anxieties? You always seem so calm."

He shrugged. "I don't know. I just live a day at a time, that's all. And things always work out. Look back on your life right now, this minute, and see if it hasn't worked out well."

"Then I guess we shouldn't worry about the future," I said.

"Live in the moment," said Arnold, "and love the moment. Because the moment is all that we have. You see, the past is dead and the future hasn't happened yet. So all we have is the now. If you believe in the now, you will never have anxieties. It's just that most people, for some reason, have a kind of death grip on the universe."

"How do you mean?"

Arnold stared at the water—at the ferry, and at two swans who were passing by. "I mean that most people don't know how to let go. So they cling to the past, and anticipate the future, and never enjoy the present. They fear death and loss—death and loss being only illusions, by the way—and so they never experience themselves for what they are. Life itself, pulsing, throbbing, breathing life. You and I, my darling, are the trees of the universe, and the flowers and the stars. We are the same as planets and moons, mice and chipmunks, and everything that has ever been created and will never die. Because the whole dance is *one* dance. Distinctions between things are simply illusions."

"Wow," I said. Because in that moment I felt a huge rush of affection for Arnold, a wave of admiration and love. And as we sat there and watched the passage of the ferry, I knew that he was right. I may not have understood all his words, but the meaning behind them was crystal clear. Arnold Bromberg was right.

I AM A TREE of the universe, I said to myself, as I pedaled along Route 114 on a secondhand bike. I am the flowers and the stars. . . . But God, what a terrible bike it was, purchased, as usual, at the thrift shop. Nevertheless. It was my mode of transportation and I was trying to be grateful for it. The police had not yet found my stolen Honda, but I had a brand-new job. With a lady author named Nora Thurston Quadrangle.

The ad had appeared in the paper just two days ago. "Wanted, young person to assist children's author with various chores. Some typing necessary. Organizational skills a must."

So I had phoned this person, who turned out to be a woman, and had pedaled over to her house, which was in a neighborhood called Redwood— just beyond the Harborside Motel. I hadn't dressed up for the interview because I figured that a lady author would be a bohemian type.

Wrong. Because rather than being a bohemian type, she looked like she had just stepped out of *Vogue*. And her house was pure *House and Garden*.

What a mistake I had made! What I mean is, I should not have worn overalls.

To begin with, her home was the kind of place my mother would have given her eyeteeth to live in—the type of house that is always included in the Sag Harbor "Historic Houses" tour every Christmas. An eighteenth-century cottage that looked out at the cove. Old, mellow, polished wood floors. Skylights. Hundreds of books, and a small Steinway piano in the living room. Vases of flowers everywhere. All of which would have been intimidating enough. But then there was Miss Quadrangle herself—the Dragon Lady.

"How do you do?" I said, when she came to the door. "I'm the girl who phoned you this morning. About the job."

Miss Quadrangle looked me over, as though I was something she was thinking of purchasing. At the hardware store. "I'm Nora Thurston Quadrangle," she said. We shook hands.

She led me into her glamorous eighteenth-century living room, and ushered me over to a glamorous eighteenth-century chair. "Do sit down," she said coolly. "What is your name?"

"Rita Formica. I live over in North Haven."

"Can you type?" asked Miss Quadrangle.

"Yes, ma'am."

"Do you mind doing housework?"

"Oh, no."

"How old are you?"

"Eighteen," I replied.

"You look younger," she said sternly.

"Yes, ma'am," I replied.

In the pause that followed, I studied Miss Quadrangle. She had short gray hair, perfectly coiffed, and she was wearing tweed slacks and a cashmere sweater. A heavy gold bracelet on one wrist. No wedding ring. I really dug her shoes, which were soft brown leather with straps across them. They probably cost a mint.

"What I'm looking for," said Miss Quadrangle, "is a person to type letters, pay my bills, and do some vacuuming and shopping. I'm very busy at the moment, getting a book ready for the publisher, and I need assistance. The job pays eight dollars an hour."

"I think I would suit you very well," I said. "My, uh, fiancé, is a writer too."

There was a very slight pause. "Would I know his name?" asked Miss Quadrangle.

"I don't think so. I mean, he has an advance on a book, but it isn't published yet."

"Do you have a car?" she inquired.

"Well, no. But I can easily come over on my bike."

"Hmmm," she said enigmatically. "Let me make us some coffee. Meanwhile, you can glance at my books. Over there, in the bookcase."

Miss Quadrangle disappeared into the kitchen, and I looked at the living room again. Paintings, a few pieces of sculpture, glass paperweights on tabletops. Lots of tapes, and a really fantastic stereo. Poor she was not.

I went over to the bookcase and took down the books she had pointed out. They were for very little kids, and all of them had the word "good" in the title. *The Good Little Eggbeater*, *The Good Little Toothbrush*, *The Good Little Vacuum Cleaner*, *The Good Little Blender*. Etc. On the front flap of *The Good Little Eggbeater*, it said, "This moving tale, by an award-winning author, tells of the adventures of an old-fashioned eggbeater who has been cast aside. When he leaves his tiny home, in search of someone who will appreciate him, little does he realize that . . ."

I turned to the back flap, where it said, "Nora Thurston Quadrangle is the author of more than thirty books for children. Her 'good little' series has won numerous awards and will soon be seen in animated form, in a group of films to be made by Loring Productions. Miss Quadrangle was born in Boston and now lives in Sag Harbor, New York."

71

Miss Quadrangle came back with the coffee and sat down opposite me. "Have you looked at the books?"

"Yes, ma'am," I said. "Uh, how did you get the idea for this appliance series? If you don't mind my asking."

Miss Quadrangle gave me a cold look. "I studied the market, of course."

I had an image of Miss Quadrangle, in her chic clothes, walking through a vegetable market. But I had a feeling that wasn't what she meant.

"The market?" I repeated. "What exactly is that, if you don't mind my asking."

"The market is what sells," she explained. "And if there's one thing I know, it's what sells. Children, you see, identify with appliances."

"They do?"

"Of course they do! Studies have been done for years on the attraction young children feel toward irons and toasters, blenders and vacuum cleaners. It may have something to do with the fact that the child is helpless and identifies with the power of machines."

I was turning the pages of *The Good Little Eggbeater* as Miss Quadrangle spoke. "Do you do the illustrations too?"

"Yes. There's no money in it otherwise. And, if

I do say so myself, in terms of sales these books are on a level with Dr. Seuss."

"Well," I said. Because that was all I could think of saying.

Miss Quadrangle gave me one of her cold looks. "Do you want the job or not?"

"Oh, yes," I said. "Yes, ma'am. I certainly do."

"Very well," she said. "The hours are one to five on weekdays, and I must insist that you come on time. I'm rather a stickler about time, and neatness, and you may find me just a little bit demanding. However, that's the way I am."

"Yes, ma'am," I said. "Of course. I'll . . . I'll see you tomorrow."

And with that, I made a speedy exit.

I *hated* Miss Quadrangle, and the more I worked for her, the more violent my hatred became. It wasn't an obscure kind of hatred. It was a crystal-clear, up-front kind of hatred that came from the fact that she was such an effing operator. I mean, my God, appliances! Good little eggbeaters, noble vacuum cleaners. And by producing this crap she was making a fortune. Arnold, whose book on Bach was so brilliant that I couldn't read parts of it without weeping, had been given an advance so tiny that it wouldn't have kept a mouse alive. And then there was me. My book. *All the Slow Dances.*

All right, I admit it. Things were beginning to get to me. Slowly, surely, day by day, things were beginning to get me down. The fact that I worked while Arnold stayed home and wrote his book. The fact that *my* book was never mentioned in our household. The fact that when I came home from working for the Dragon Lady, Arnold would be down on the beach, photographing swans. He had bought himself an old camera—at the thrift shop, where else—and was deeply into bird photography now. Swans, herons, and cormorants. Mallard ducks.

Any feminist in the world—my friend Corry Brown, for example—would have said that my situation was wrong. Because not only was I the wage earner in our household, I also did the grocery shopping, took the laundry to town, and chopped wood for the fire—Arnold having a bad back. Arnold did cook dinner, but he used every pot and pan in the house while doing so. *I* did the dishes.

The difference in our life-styles was beginning to be apparent. I mean, Arnold is a person who likes to rise at dawn and go walking on the beach—whereas I am a late sleeper. Someone who has to be pulled out of bed in the morning and who can't function until the third cup of coffee. Arnold is very neat. I am not. And Arnold, I discovered, wanted to make love every single night of his life—which for me was a little excessive.

I was getting angrier and angrier—because we had no car, no radio, no television and no heat. Because we had no bathtub and had to bathe in a little "hip bath" that Arnold had found at a junk store. It also annoyed me that the roof leaked onto our bed whenever the rain came from the east. In addition, the stove did not work well and the refrigerator made a noise like someone coughing. I would wake in the middle of the night, think that Arnold was coughing, and it would be the refrigerator. I should give this idea to Miss Quadrangle, I thought. *The Good Little Coughing Refrigerator*.

One afternoon, after leaving the Dragon Lady's house, I did a strange thing. I rode my bike over to Clarence Street and parked it at a distance from Tony's Auto Repair. And there was my dad, watching one of his mechanics work on a Mercedes, standing there with a cigar in his mouth, paunchy as ever—but older somehow, and more tired. He was telling the mechanic how to do something under the car, and he was being patient about it, but God, how tired and defeated he looked. Much older than his thirty-eight years.

I stood there for a long time, watching him— and then I realized how much I missed him. It was early November now, and I had missed him very much. I love you, Daddy, I said silently. And then I turned my bike toward home.

12

ARNOLD AND I were quarreling. Or rather, *I* was quarreling and Arnold was listening. A pained and worried look on his face, he sat on the edge of our bed as I complained about 1) our lack of material possessions 2) our bank balance 3) R.W. Moss.

More about R.W. Moss in a minute.

The thing is, it is very hard to fight with Arnold. He listens and nods his head—but underneath it all you can see how hurt he is, how bewildered. Seeing no issues in our lives, Arnold could not fight over them. Acknowledging no problems, he felt there was nothing to solve. "Things aren't fair here," I said. "I mean, all you do is write a few pages of your book every day and then fool around on the beach. I hate that Quadrangle woman—and my legs are almost paralyzed from riding that goddam bike to town. Do you think I like writing 'Hospital News,' describing the new gift shop in the lobby? *I'm* a writer too, and yet my book just lies in the bureau."

Arnold shook his head, bewildered. "I have never wanted to keep you from writing. You write beautifully."

"But you *are* keeping me from writing! How can I write? I've got too much to do."

"Get up earlier. Write at six in the morning."

"At six in the morning I am asleep," I said between clenched teeth. "And the reason I am asleep at six in the morning is that we make love until three in the morning. You, Arnold, take a nap every afternoon. I do not. The whole thing is unfair."

"When was life ever fair?" Arnold mused.

"Arnold, look. Every morning I work on 'Hospital News.' And then I work for the Dragon Lady. And then I do groceries and laundry. And then I come home and chop wood. I'm not a pioneer woman, Arnold. We're not crossing the plains."

He rose to his feet and walked over to the window. It was nine at night, and the ferry was gliding through the autumn fog. "Your words hurt me," he said.

"I can't get anywhere with you! It's like trying to fight with a corpse."

"But why should we fight at all?"

"I'm going down to the beach," I said. "And I'm going to sit there all night. Because I am in a rage, Arnold, and even though I'm trying to explain the whole thing to you, you won't listen. Life is not a metaphysical exercise! Life is not philosophy! Life is paying the rent and needing a car, and wanting an effing bathtub. Is it too much to want a bathtub, Arnold? Too much to want to bathe?"

I didn't give him a chance to reply, because I had already stormed out of the house and was taking

77

the path to the beach. I felt both angry and guilty, and I had a strong desire to spend the whole night on the beach in the freezing November weather. Yes. I wanted to catch pneumonia and die and have Arnold regret his incredible attitudes and everything he had ever done to me.

But what, really, had he done?

I sat down on the cold sand and watched the ferry glide toward Shelter Island. Its lights were glowing softly in the fog, amorphous, unreal. Somewhere in the woods behind me an owl was hooting. The usual nightly panorama of stars was absent. Even though I was wearing a heavy sweater and jeans, I was cold.

One of my problems these days was R.W. Moss. But to mention R.W. was to get into real trouble with Arnold, because R.W. was his new and beloved friend.

Spending so much time on the beach, Arnold had discovered that right by the ferry there is a little booth, sort of like a tollbooth, and that inside this booth sat an old man named R.W. Moss. His job was simply to let down the gangplank when the ferry came in—and pull up the gangplank when the ferry went out. The rest of the time, summer and winter, in fair weather and foul, R.W. stayed inside his booth. He had an electric heater in there, and a radio, and a coffeemaker, and this was his life. Sitting in a tollbooth, putting a gangplank up and down.

Well. Upon discovering R.W. Moss, Arnold had almost fallen apart. Such a lonely job the man had! And he was at least seventy! Such a brave person Mr. Moss was, to sit there winter and summer, alone, listening to the radio. At least he *has* a radio, I had replied, which is more than we do. But that, said Arnold, wasn't the point. The point was that down on the beach, just a few yards from our house, sat an old man in a tollbooth. Cold and lonely. Hungry, perhaps. And so he invited him up to the house.

By the end of November, I felt like I had two housemates. Arnold and R.W. Moss. I mean, my God, he was in our house every evening—he got off work at five—and the thing about R.W. was that he ate a lot. No matter what Arnold had fixed for dinner, R.W. ate most of it—and this got to be quite a sore point with me. "Arnold," I said, one frosty November morning, "R.W. Moss is eating all of our food. It isn't right."

Arnold looked at me, amazed. "Would you begrudge another human being *food*?" he asked.

And what do you reply to that? Yes, indeed, I do begrudge my fellow creatures food, especially if the food is mine. Yes, I begrudge them every bite.

79

R.W. Moss was tiny and bald. He had the red nose of a heavy drinker, and he had once been a sea captain. Which of course was the thing that enchanted Arnold. R.W. had been to sea in the old days, and had many a yarn to tell. About rounding Cape Horn. About sailing to Australia. About opium dens in Hong Kong. So he continued to eat with us, at least six nights a week, and I continued to complain. Because he was eating all of the food.

I sat there on the sand that night, getting colder and colder, and somewhere inside of me was a feeling that made me a little sick. It was a feeling that maybe my parents had been right. I had given up a normal life for Arnold Bromberg, and what had I gotten in return? A house without heat that overlooked a ferry. A secondhand bike. R.W. Moss. All over America girls my age were in their first year of college, or if they weren't, they were preparing for careers. Or, if they weren't doing *that*, they were having babies and becoming domestic. But I wasn't doing any of these things, and suddenly it scared me. Who was this person called Rita Formica, and what would she become?

I sat on the beach until midnight. And then, stiff and cold, I went back to the house. Arnold was asleep, but he had left a light burning for me, and pinned to my pillow was a note in his handwriting.

No, not exactly a note. It was a poem by Ezra Pound.

> Be in me as the eternal moods
>   of the bleak wind, and not
> As transient things are—
>   gaiety of flowers.
> Have me in the strong loneliness
>   of sunless cliffs
> And of gray waters,
>   Let the gods speak softly of us
> In days hereafter,
>   The shadowy flowers of Orcus
> Remember thee.

13

"THE CONTRACTS ARE in one file," the Dragon Lady was saying, "and the royalty statements are in another. Film options and foreign sales, of course, are kept separately. Do you understand?"

"Oh, yes," I said briskly. "Yes, ma'am. Absolutely."

"I am rather a stickler about my files," Miss Quadrangle stated. "They are very important to me."

And so is your bank account, I thought. Wow,

lady, you really are a money machine. I wouldn't have believed it.

OK, so I was jealous. I admit it. Because I would have given my soul to be published—and for Arnold to be published—while here was this children's book factory named Nora Thurston Quadrangle, turning out books by the dozen and making a mint. I will say, however, that she was disciplined about it. Nothing got in the way of the Dragon Lady's schedule.

Nora Thurston Quadrangle—thought of by me as the Dragon Lady, or sometimes as the Quad—rose at dawn every morning and went to her workroom, a beautiful place with a skylight, that faced the cove. There, with a thermos of coffee at hand, she worked until I arrived at one P.M. So many hours for text, so many hours for illustrations, and no answering the phone. The phone had an answering machine attached to it, the stereo worked on remote control, and her IBM typewriter, and charcoals, and watercolors, were all arranged on a kind of wraparound desk. A huge desk, made of blond wood.

I had to admire it all, even though it made me furious. Because the Quad worked very hard. But at *what* did she work hard, that was the question. At a lot of stupid books that had appliances for heros. Angelic steam irons. Unselfish blenders.

Electric toothbrushes who had fits of nostalgia for the old days. The good old days, when toothbrushes had been on Manual. God, I thought, how fantastic to devote one's creativity to such junk. And yet the Quad made heaps and heaps of money.

It was apparent in her clothes, which were pure Saks Fifth Avenue. It was apparent in her car—an old Bentley—and in her jewelry, which was so understated that it had to be expensive. It was particularly apparent in the fact that her hairdresser, a delicate boy named Shawn, came to her instead of her going to him. Every Wednesday Shawn would drift over to Redwood, all twinkles and smiles, and do Madame's hair. While he clipped and coiffed, I would type the Quad's letters, or do her filing, or go out for groceries. Once a week, I vacuumed her house from top to bottom, and because it was December now, I was also shoveling her snow.

There were lots of phone calls from editors. There were lots of letters asking her to speak at library functions and book fairs. There were prizes, and foreign sales, and her books coming out in paperback editions—and all of it made me a little ill.

But one significant thing had happened—which is that Arnold had taken a job. Yes. The very morning after I had found that poem pinned to my pillow, he had walked all the way to Sag Harbor and found employment. Now I grant you that it wasn't a hell of a job. I mean, it was only playing the organ in an Episcopal church two Sundays a month—the real organist being in failing health—but at least it was something. At least it showed the *intention* of making money. Two Sundays a month, Arnold sat in an organ loft and played Bach and Handel, Corelli and Buxtehude. And of course, on those two Sundays I went to church with him.

I had recently heard the Quad use the words "Renaissance Man" to describe a friend of hers in the city. "Yes," said the Quad to me, "Peter is a Renaissance Man. He does everything." I was beginning to think that Arnold was like that too. I mean, there was very little Arnold could not do—except make money—and unlike me, he seemed to have no mental blocks. Wanting to be a photographer, he simply bought an old camera and became one. Wanting to paint the ferry, he bought a little set of watercolors and did some wonderful pictures. If a poem was needed for an occasion, he could write one. If someone needed a birthday cake, he could bake it.

But we still fought. I mean, *I* fought while he listened sadly. Because I just didn't know how long I could continue to commute to town on a second-hand bike. It was snowing now, and there I was every day, riding the bike three miles into town and three miles back. Also, my boss at Hampton

Hospital, Mr. Parish, had told me that "Hospital News" made very dull reading these days. "Can't you spice it up?" he asked. "Can't you make it more colorful?"

So I tried to write more wittily about the new gift shop, and the fact that the cafeteria would soon be painted pink. It was blue, but soon it would be pink. The Ladies' Improvement Committee had decided this.

"The difference between blue and pink is a big one," I wrote, "pink being a *much* more cheerful color than blue. Your vigilant reporter has learned that the Ladies' Committee is even having the particular paint mixed to order, so that the tones of pink will blend in with the draperies Mrs. Hamburger is having made. The idea is to have the cafeteria look more like a dining room than a cafeteria. The idea is to provide the staff with true relaxation."

"I am rather a stickler about my files," Miss Quadrangle was saying. "They are very important to me."

It was snowing outside, and the Quad was having a cup of coffee while I did her filing. After the filing, I would type the letters she had put on the dictating machine. And after the letters, I would trudge out into the snow and do her grocery shopping. This evening she was having a dinner party. Special Occasions, in Bridgehampton, was catering it, and *I* was serving it. I just hoped that I wouldn't drop food on the guests.

I had begun to realize—slowly, steadily—that I was not the first person who had worked for the Quad. She would let slip little references to Milly, who had been into the sherry all the time, and Sandra, who had stolen money from her purse. There was also someone named Betsy, who had gotten pregnant and departed—and a man named Wilmore. What had happened to Wilmore, I could not imagine, but I thought the entire group had been lucky to escape. The Quad was not just a stickler about things, she was a fanatic. About dust, about punctuality, about her perfectly balanced checkbook, and her perfectly filed files.

As I pulled on my wool cap and duffle coat, and headed for the IFA grocery store, I felt a wave of depression wash over me. Not long ago it had been Thanksgiving—and instead of going to my family, Arnold and I had spent the evening with R.W. Moss, or "the Captain," as Arnold called him.

About three days before the holiday, I had received a Thanksgiving card from my father, a garish one with a big orange turkey on the front. Inside the card it said, "Happy Gobble Day." And, in my father's large handwriting, was this message.

"Honey, we want you to come home for Thanksgiving dinner because life is pretty lonely here without our girl. If you want to come, your mother is serving the meal at four. Your loving Dad."

No mention of Arnold, not even one word. So I had sent a card back saying no thank you. And then Arnold and I had gotten up early on Thanksgiving Day, to cook a sumptuous meal for Captain Moss. Not a turkey, because we couldn't afford that, but a nice roast chicken with stuffing and vegetables. A bottle of red wine. Arnold's homemade apple pie. But all through the day I had felt waves of sadness washing over me—just as they were doing now—because it was the first Thanksgiving of my life without my parents.

One night, very late, lying beside Arnold after we had made love—and after he had fallen asleep—I realized something. Arnold was only four years younger than my parents, who were both thirty-eight. In other words, he was their generation—and this gave me pause for thought. When I had first met him, the thing that had shocked my mother the most was Arnold's age. But what my mother didn't know was that I had always been attracted to older people. With the exception of a violent crush I had once had on a jock named Robert Swann, I had never been attracted to anyone remotely my own age. When had all this started, this feeling of alienation from my peers? Probably in the first grade, when we had had that goddam school play.

It was springtime, I was just completing the first grade, and Miss Bumpers, the teacher, had decided to put on a little play for Parents' Day called "The Flight of the Moths." It was all about these moths who get born, or hatched or whatever, only to live briefly and die. The whole class would be costumed in gauzy outfits and do a little ballet—except for me, of course. *I* was too fat, too tubby, to be a moth—and so, after watching me dance with the other kids during rehearsal, Miss Bumpers took me aside. "Rita, dear," she said, "I don't think you make a good moth. I think we'll give you a special part called the Mothball."

"The what?" I said.

"The Mothball, dear. A special part created just for *you*."

So Miss Bumpers made me a costume out of white terrycloth, complete with a hood through which you could only see my eyes, and I became the Mothball—the enemy of the whole ballet, the villain who would kill some of the poor moths prematurely, sending them to an early grave. Well. You can imagine how popular this made me with the other first graders, how admired and loved. And would you believe it? The name "Mothball" stuck with me all the way through grammar school. . . . This, of course, is only one example of a thousand kinds of loneliness and a thousand kinds of alienation. But hell. Why shouldn't I have started liking older people? Why shouldn't I have opted out?

That evening, December 5th, the Quad had her dinner party—and I served it. I, in a dress and apron, in stockings and patent leather shoes, I who had curled my hair and put on lipstick, served dinner to five of the most asinine people God ever created.

To begin with, the Quad was very nervous about this party, very uptight. I mean, you would have thought Prince Charles and Diana were coming. You would have thought we were serving drinks to Liz Taylor. The flowers on the dining table had to be just right, and the lighting had to be just right, and a cheery fire had to be burning in the fireplace, and mulled wine had to be served correctly in big glass mugs. The Quad, who is not exactly a feminine person, wore a long wool skirt and a white silk blouse and some of her understated jewelry.

The guests were two local couples—stuffy, rich—and one elderly decorator named Jeffrey. Why these particular people made the Quad so nervous, I could not imagine, because they were dull dull dull. I almost fell asleep during the cocktail hour, listening to them talk about real estate and dog shows. I had to stifle yawns while serving them dinner, as they discussed Nancy Reagan's wardrobe and the high cost of health care. Jeffrey, the ancient decorator, whose gray hair was tinted blond, kept saying things like, "But I do think *angst* and anxiety are different things, don't you?" And at one point, apropos of nothing, he said, "A *true* mauve is so hard to find these days. I've almost given up."

On and on. Through my perfectly served main course, and into my perfectly served dessert. I did not drop food on anyone. I kept the wine glasses filled. Beef Wellington, and endive salad, and fresh strawberries with Cointreau. I brought in the tray with the coffeepot and demitasse cups. I rinsed the dishes and put them in the dishwasher, and then I was ready to go.

The Quad, surprisingly, was a little tight. She walked me to the back door and stood there for a moment. "It's a *very* good party, don't you think?" she said.

"Oh, yes," I said. "Very."

"I think they're having a good time."

"Yes, ma'am. They really are."

"Jeffrey's such a dear."

"He is," I said. "Adorable."

"You did a good job," said the Quad, swaying a little. "You want a little nip before you go?"

For one moment, I couldn't imagine what she meant. Then I realized that she meant booze.

"No thank you," I said. "Good night, Miss Quadrangle."

I had changed back into my blue jeans, and a sweater, and my duffle coat. And now I had a three-mile ride home in the bitter cold. And as I pedaled along Route 114, I felt like giving up. I mean, what was life all about, when people like the Dragon Lady had such good luck, and people like Arnold and me had such bad luck.

But is she happy? a voice inside of me said. She's rich, but is she happy?

Well no, said another voice, she isn't. Because she's lonely and insecure, and maybe drinks too much, and has to have friends like that awful Jeffrey. But she's made it, the Quad has, and that's what our culture is always telling you to do. You've got to *make it*, before old age or cancer sets in. You've got to be rich, or famous, or both.

Why? said the first voice.

The second voice was stumped for a moment, but finally it said, Because that's the consensus of opinion, you dope. Rich and thin is better than poor and fat. A Bentley is better than a bicycle. It is comforting to have central heating in the winter. Regular meals are fun.

Halfway home on the bicycle, it started to snow again—and when I say snow, I mean a blizzard. Suddenly, I couldn't see the road, and the cars that were passing me were passing too close. I got off the bike and decided to walk it home. Thirty minutes later, I entered the Ferry House. My clothes were caked with snow, and my eyebrows were caked with snow, and I could no longer feel my feet. In front of the wood fire, Arnold and the Captain were drinking wine together. The remains of a meat loaf lay on the dinner table. The dishes were unwashed.

"Darling!" said Arnold cheerfully. "There you are. You must be frozen. Do you want a cup of tea?"

I looked at the Captain, who was plastered, and felt such anger that I could not speak. "Hello there, my darlin'," said the Captain. "How's the girl?"

I WENT OVER and stood by the stove, to get warm. I peeled off my snow-laden garments. "The Captain was just telling me about the time he was kidnapped in Hong Kong," Arnold explained.

The Captain leaned back in his chair. "Yep," he

said, "kidnapped in Hong Kong. Trapped in a den of thieves and then kidnapped. How I ever got out of *that* one alive, I do not know. Mercy on us! And all because of a girl named Chee Ling. Beautiful she was, but a liar. Led me on with sweet and pretty words, but she was really leading me to my doom. Outnumbered I was too, ten to one. And then Chee Ling ran off to her parents' home. *They*, you see, was royalty of the old kind. Ancient Chinese royalty."

I stood there dripping by the stove, as the Captain continued his story. Arnold, of course, was hanging on to every word. It was like having deep and utter faith in an old John Wayne movie. Incredible.

"Blindfolded me, they did," said the Captain. "And then, before I knew it, I'm on a vessel of some kind. A ship, veering and pitching through the waves. Mercy on us! I was a goner for sure, and Chee Ling a traitor. 'Where are the diamonds?' the leader of the gang said to me. 'Reveal where they are, or we cut your throat!' "

"Mr. Moss," I said, "I'm sorry to interrupt you, but I have to go to bed."

R.W. Moss shook his head from side to side, as though he were coming out of a dream. "What's that, little lady?"

"Bed," I repeated. "I have to go to bed. So I'm afraid I must ask you to leave."

All the color seemed to drain from Arnold's face. "But Rita . . ."

"I'm sorry, Arnold. But since we do not have a bedroom here, to which I can withdraw, I have to ask Mr. Moss to go. I've just walked a mile through a snowstorm and I'm shivering."

R.W. Moss rose unsteadily to his feet. "Of course, little lady, of course. You get some shut-eye now. I'll finish the tale tomorrow."

Looking embarrassed, Arnold walked R.W. Moss to the door. "Can you make it home through the snow?" he asked. But it was an irrelevant question, because R.W. only lived a few yards down the road. In a cottage on someone's estate.

"Take care, sir," Arnold said to the Captain. "I'll see you tomorrow."

"Blessings on ye," said R.W. And then he was gone.

Arnold turned to confront me. I was already pulling off my clothes and getting into my pajamas. "How could you have done that?" he said.

I pulled on my pajama top and got into bed. "Done what, Arnold?"

"Asked him to *leave*. How could you have been so rude?"

"Arnold," I said in a steely voice, "our bedroom is also our living room. I had no other choice."

"But Rita, he's an old man. . . ."

"Yes," I said, "and I will soon be an old woman. Sooner than you know."

"I've never seen you behave that way before. You are usually so considerate."

I wriggled down under the covers. "You know something, Arnold? Once, just once, I would like someone to be considerate of *me*. I mean, I have just walked through a snowstorm, and I already feel like I'm getting a cold, and yet all you can talk of is the Captain. An old drunk who bores the pants off me."

Arnold looked shocked. "R.W. Moss is not an old drunk."

"Then what would you call it?"

"He's just a dreamer, that's all."

"He is also a bloody liar. None of those stories are true."

Arnold sighed and walked over to the wood stove. He opened the little door and stirred the coals around. "I don't want to fight with you," he said.

"And *I* don't want to sound like a shrew. All I sound like these days is a shrew."

"Do you want a hot drink? A toddy of some kind?"

I turned over on my side. "No. I just want to sleep."

But he did not join me in bed. He just sat there by the stove for a long time, staring at the coals, and I knew I had hurt him badly. I had hurt him to the core, but there wasn't a thing I could do about it.

The next morning, I did indeed have a cold. A terrible cold, the worst of my life, so that I could not go to work. Arnold phoned Miss Quadrangle with the news. Then he busied himself making fresh juice, and brewing herb teas. At nine thirty, he went down to the ferry to borrow R.W.'s radio.

"The Captain was glad to loan you his radio," said Arnold, brushing the snow off his boots. "He said to keep it as long as you like."

"Good, good," I muttered, feeling stuffed up and miserable. "I'll listen to some music."

It's funny, but it had been so long since I had played a radio, or a TV set, that I was almost glad I had gotten sick. For the first part of the morning, I listened to music on FM. Then, around noon, I switched over to something on AM called "The Susan Goforth Show." It was instant psychotherapy, done over the radio. And it was fascinating.

Because it was a daytime show, most of Dr. Goforth's callers were housewives. I sipped my orange juice and listened, as Arnold stirred the chicken soup he was making.

"Dr. Goforth, my name is Anne," said one caller, "and I'm really unhappy. I hope you can help me."

"Go on, Anne," said Dr. Goforth. "I'm listening."

"I'm forty years old," said Anne, "and my kids are grown and everything, and my husband is faithful to me, so I don't know why I should feel so awful. But it's like the caller before me said: Is this all there is? I mean, I look back on my life, and I wonder what it was about."

"I'm listening, Anne. Go on."

"I did all the right things," said Anne. "I mean, I married a nice guy, and had two kids, and we moved to the suburbs and everything. And then I joined the PTA, and my husband joined the Rotary Club, and we gave dinner parties and developed a group of wonderful friends. We had a dog named Rascal, and my mother would come to visit twice a year from Florida. My mother and my husband get along, you know. There's no conflict there."

"I'm listening. But I need to know what your question is, Anne. Our time is short."

"I don't *know* what my question is, doctor. It's just that I feel I did everything right—I mean, I baked all the cookies, and gave birthday parties, and drove the kids everywhere, to every kind of activity in the world—and I still love my husband. But there's such an emptiness inside."

"Anne," said Dr. Goforth, "our time is running

97

out. Tell me, what did you want to be when you were young? In your teens."

There was a pause. "Well," said Anne, "I . . . I wanted to be a clown."

"What?"

"A clown, Dr. Goforth, in the circus. I wanted to be a clown."

That one, obviously, had the doctor stumped. "Well, for goodness' sake," she said. "That's very unusual."

"I know," said Anne miserably, "that was the trouble. It was *too* unusual. People thought I was crazy. But that's what I wanted to be. A clown with a big outfit like Ringling Brothers or something. A clown who would make people laugh."

"I'm sorry, Anne, but we're out of time," said Dr. Goforth. "Good luck to you, and thanks for calling."

I switched off the radio. "Arnold," I said, "that woman wanted to be a clown. When she was young, I mean."

"Hmmm?" said Arnold, who was deeply involved at the stove. "What, darling?"

"Nothing," I said, but for the rest of the day, as I went through two boxes of Kleenex, and kept taking aspirin and juice, I just kept thinking of Anne. Poor wonderful Anne—who had wanted to be a clown.

15

ALL THROUGH THE MONTH of December, I thought about Anne. In fact, I thought about Anne so much that I could even see her. She was a big woman, a cheerful type who made a good neighbor and a good friend, and the kind who belonged to all the local clubs and had her hair done on Saturday mornings. She had been a good mother too, and a loyal wife, but all these years—when she lay in bed beside her husband, or did the laundry—all these years the image of her young self, in a clown suit, had haunted her mind.

Anne would stand by the washing machine, as it hummed away, and in her mind would be the most wonderful circus in the world. A three-ring circus with elephants and bareback riders, and trapeze artists, and little dogs who did tricks. There she would be—in an incredible clown suit, her nose red and bulbous, a fright wig on her head, running around the ring with all the other clowns, tumbling, pratfalling, making people laugh.

And why did a person want to be a clown? Because she already felt so ridiculous, and lonely, that she needed to put all that emotion into something positive. Anne, I thought, I dig the whole thing. Because you should have been a clown, no matter what. To hell with the husband and the kids, and to hell with the goddam suburbs. Anne, old buddy, you should have done it.

A week before Christmas, Arnold was scheduled to give an organ concert at the Epispocal church. The event had been mentioned in the paper, in a column called "Sag Harbor News," and I was very excited for him. And, because I had been out of touch with my mother since that unfortunate tea party, I clipped out the newspaper article and sent it to her with a note. "I hope you'll come to hear Arnold play on the 18th," I said. "He's really good."

Crazy. To live in a small town and never bump into them—my parents, I mean. To go to the grocery store, and the dry cleaner's, one eye always peeled, but never seeing them at all. You'd have to know Sag Harbor to know what I mean, but it really is an intimate kind of place. With the exception of the summers, when we are flooded with tourists, our town is very quiet and friendly. A place where people say good morning to you on the street, even if they don't know you personally—a place with a volunteer fire department, and a volunteer ambulance corps. If you stand at the top of Main Street and look down toward the harbor, what you see are a lot of plain little shops, and an old-fashioned Municipal Building, and an ancient hotel. At the very end of this street is a windmill—and then just the harbor, and water, and boats.

On the evening of December 18th, Arnold got dressed in his one good dark-blue suit, and a maroon tie. Polished black shoes, a maroon handkerchief in his breast pocket, his bushy hair slicked back. He really looked elegant, if I do say so myself, and because I didn't want him to walk to town, or ride our miserable bike, I got one of the neighbors to drive us there. By seven thirty that evening the church was beginning to fill up.

I was surprised at how many people came—and surprised particularly at how many young people came. In ones and twos, they filed quietly into the church, which was decorated with pine boughs. Yes, there was Mr. and Mrs. Gerard, who ran the IFA grocery store, and there was the Scott family, who I had known all my life. The whole town seemed to be coming to Arnold's concert—but not my mom.

I sat far in the back, so I could see her if she came in, but there was no sign of her. And to say that I was disappointed is the understatement of the year. As the church filled up, and as I realized that she wasn't coming, I felt tears begin inside of me. What was life all about, when she wouldn't even do this for me? Wouldn't even come to a concert.

Arnold stepped into the organ loft and stood there for a moment, looking very distinguished. There was a scattering of applause. He nodded, and sat down at the organ. The church, suddenly, was quiet.

He began with an old Christmas melody and then dovetailed into a beautiful piece by Bach. He had discussed the program with me many times, the idea being to weave old Christmas carols in and out of Bach and Handel. It was a lovely idea, and now that I was able to hear it, I knew he had been right. And, my God, how well he played now. *Much* better than when I had met him two years ago. More confidence, more power. With the exception of the organist at the Fraumunster cathedral, in Zurich, there was nobody in the world who could play the organ like Arnold. As I listened to him, a chill went down my spine.

Everyone in that church had his face uplifted to the music. It was so beautiful, so spontaneous, the way people were reacting. Oh Arnold, I thought, you really are a Renaissance Man. It's true.

And then my mother came in.

She stole in very quietly and sat down in a back pew. And, because I was sitting on the other side of the church, she didn't see me. But I was so glad to see *her* that I wanted to shout, or wave or something. None of which I did, of course. As Arnold's music filled the air, swelling and building like steps of gold, my mother raised her face to the music and listened.

I watched her, moved to tears. Because I knew that she was hearing the beauty of it and hearing the skill involved. Arnold was playing parts of *Messiah* now, and the playing was brilliant.

He ended the concert with the "Hallelujah Chorus" from *Messiah*—and when he came to a triumphant halt, there was absolute silence in the church. Then—in a body—the audience rose to its feet and began to applaud. In one wave they were on their feet, and a man next to me even shouted "Bravo!" Oh God, it was so wonderful. And I knew that my mother was digging the whole thing too. As the applause continued, she left the church—but I knew that she had seen Arnold up there, bowing modestly, a little surprised by the commotion he had caused. I knew she had seen how wonderful he looked.

That night, as Arnold and I celebrated with a bottle of wine, and some cheese and crackers, it was like the old days. The days when we had first met and fallen in love. I toasted Arnold in front of the wood stove, and he toasted me, and then we went to bed together. I snuggled up against him and kissed his cheek. "You were so wonderful," I whispered. "I was so proud of you."

"I love you, Rita," said Arnold Bromberg. "Forever."

THEN, ALL TOO SOON, it was Christmas Eve, and I was in a slough of depression. Slough, pit, trench—you name it, I was in it. Because it was Christmas and Arnold and I were poorer than ever. Too poor for presents, and too poor to decorate our tree. Like a real country person, Arnold had tramped into the woods to chop down a tree for us, but we had no ornaments and wound up decorating it with cutout pieces of construction paper. Humming cheerfully, Arnold cut out angels and teddy bears, hearts and flowers, but I myself was depressed.

I was depressed by the fact that I was still riding a rusty bike back and forth to town, and depressed by the fact that I now took things from people's garbage cans without blinking an eye. Anything that could be of use to us, I took. Old, burnt cooking pots. A broken end table. An out-of-commission TV.

I was also depressed because I had been caught stealing a hot-water bottle from the dime store. I mean, I am NOT a thief, and the only thing I had ever stolen before was candy, when I was little, but I was very much in need of a hot-water bottle because my back was hurting from chopping wood. So I walked into the dime store one morning and concealed a large, red hot-water bottle inside my coat. But alas, on the way out of the store, someone bumped into me, and the bottle dropped out of my clothing and fell to the floor with a plop. Everyone stared—me, the woman at the cash register, and, in particular, the owner of the dime store. The trouble was that I knew him. Mr. Dodds.

"Why, Rita," said Mr. Dodds. "What has just fallen out of your coat? A hot-water bottle?"

I felt my face grow as red as the awful bottle. "What?" I said. "Excuse me?"

Mr. Dodds picked up the bottle and stared at it. "It's our ten-dollar hot-water bottle. Our best one. It was in your coat."

"My *coat*?" I repeated. "Surely you are mistaken, Mr. Dodds."

"No," he said sadly, "it was in your coat. I saw it. You were trying to steal it."

For some reason, I lost my temper at that moment. Which was not the wisest thing to do. "Well, Mr. Dodds," I said, "if you really think I was stealing one of your hot-water bottles, then you better call the cops. Or the FBI or something. Get out the handcuffs. Get a warrant for arrest."

On and on. To the point where Mr. Dodds just wanted to forget the whole thing and get me out of the store. But would I *let* him forget the whole thing? No. I just kept going on and on about it until he gave me the goddam hot-water bottle as a Christmas present.

I had sent my parents a Christmas card, signed by both Arnold and myself. They had sent one back, and that was all. No present, no check, no nothing. And it seemed very cruel.

Then there was the Dragon Lady, who—the day before Christmas—approached me with a brightly wrapped package in her hand. "I have a little present for you," she said kindly. I looked at the gift she was holding, wondering what it might be. What I was really hoping for, of course, was money. Crass of me, but that's the way I am. From time to time that week I had had a fantasy that the Quad would give me fifty dollars or something. A bonus.

"Yes," said the Quad, "I have a little present for you." She handed me a flat package, wrapped in expensive paper.

I sat down on a chair in the hallway. "That's very nice of you, Miss Quadrangle. To think of me, I mean."

The Quad, who had had a few toddies that day, smiled happily. "I hope you'll like it."

I removed the gift paper and found . . . no, not a check for fifty dollars. And not even a warm scarf, which I could have used. Nor did I find anything to eat in the package, or anything to drink. What

I found instead was one of the Quad's books. A new one, titled *The Good Little Shoe Polisher*. "I hope you'll enjoy it," said the Quad. "And your fiancé too, of course."

Why, of course he'll enjoy it, I felt like saying. Arnold always reads books labeled "Ages 5 to 8."

I opened the book to the first page. "Sammy, the electric shoe polisher, was lonely," said the text. "He had been sitting in the closet all day and . . ."

"How nice," I said falsely. "A book."

The Quad laughed—a rare occurrence. "I didn't know *what* to get you, and so I decided on this. The book is autographed, of course."

"Of course," I said. "Of course. Well. Thank you."

The Quad walked me to the door, still smiling. I had worked hard for her that day—preparing canapés for a cocktail party she was giving in a few hours, cleaning the house from top to bottom, putting more ornaments on the all-white Christmas tree. Yes, folks, an all-white tree with all-white ornaments. White, for purity.

"I hope you have a *wonderful* Christmas," said the Quad. "I hope it's everything you dream of."

I thought of the small chicken Arnold had bought for Christmas dinner. I thought of the crooked little tree with its paper ornaments. "Oh, I will," I said. "I'm sure I will."

As I pedaled home through the snow, I felt like someone out of Dickens. One of those characters who turn out to be heirs or heiresses in the end. One of those people who have to go through every kind of misfortune before they succeed. "Come off it," I said aloud. "You're just being petulant. You have Arnold for Christmas. The Quad has no one."

That thought made me feel better, in the same way that an old saying of my mother's used to make me feel better. "I cried because I had no shoes," Mom would say, "until I met a man who had no feet." Well, strangely enough, that statement always cheered me up when I was little. Most kids would find it depressing, but I would instantly become grateful for my feet, and go and wash them and put nail polish on the toes. Then I would think of the poor man who *had* no feet and make up a story about him. His feet had been devoured by a shark. He had fallen into a steel trap, while hunting, and had to shoot them off himself. He had developed gangrene in the jungles of India. On and on—this daydreaming, according to Arnold, being the hallmark of the fiction writer.

In a week it will be New Year's, I said to myself. And my New Year's resolution is to work on my book. I will get up at six every morning and work on my book if it kills me. You can't be a writer unless you write.

I had never told the Quad about my writing. Which was crazy. I mean, here was a woman who could open doors for me someday, and I had never said a word. Nor would I, I decided. I would make it on my own.

I thought of the Quad's all-white Christmas tree, and shuddered, and pedaled harder. Tomorrow was Christmas.

On Christmas morning, Arnold and I woke and embraced each other. It was our first Christmas in our own home. "I'm so happy, so happy," Arnold said as he washed his face in the kitchen sink, as he combed his curly hair. "I'll make the coffee."

Arnold's present to me, he explained, was down the road at the Captain's house. "How come?" I asked curiously. "What is it?"

"You'll see, you'll see," Arnold said happily, as he got dressed.

My present to Arnold was under the tree. A strange present, but one that I thought showed imagination. I had put a twenty-dollar deposit down on an electric typewriter, and my present was a drawing of the typewriter with the words "Coming in March!" underneath. By March, I figured, I would have it paid for.

I have failed to mention here that the middle finger on Arnold's right hand was bent out of shape, the result of a childhood accident. Because of this small deformity, typing hurt him, especially if the typewriter was not electric. So my plan was to have a Smith-Corona portable for him by spring. Oddly enough, playing the organ did *not* hurt Arnold's finger. But then, when he played the organ he was in another world.

"Open your present," I said. "I can't wait."

He brought us both mugs of coffee, stoked the fire in the wood stove, and came and sat down with me by the tree. The Captain had loaned us his radio for the holidays, and Arnold turned the dial until he got some Christmas music. "I'm so happy," he said again. Then he opened his present.

Well. You would have thought that it was the Hope diamond or something. Or a Rolls Royce. He studied the card, with its crude drawing of a typewriter, and then he burst into tears. "Oh Arnold," I said, "darling. Don't cry. It's just a typewriter. Or at least, the promise of one."

"How thoughtful of you," he said. "How imaginative."

"I'll have it for you by March. It'll save your bad finger."

"What a wonderful idea!"

"It *should* have been a word processor. But we're not that rich."

Arnold smiled. "Can you see me using a word processor?"

I smiled too. "No. I guess not."

He brushed the tears from his eyes, stood up, and ran one hand through his hair. "I'm going down the road to the Captain's house. I want to get your present."

In the fifteen minutes during which he was gone, I made the bed, got dressed, and put some sweet rolls in the oven to warm. How crazy I had been to get depressed over this Christmas, I told myself. It was the nicest Christmas of my life.

At that moment, Arnold walked through the door with a puppy.

At first I could only stare. But yes, it was a puppy— a huge one, a kind of mongrel—who was wriggling and yelping. Arnold put him down on the floor and he began to run around like crazy, wagging his tail. The point is, he was the biggest puppy I had ever seen in my life. All I could think of was how much he would eat.

"Arnold!" I said. "My God, what have you done?"

"There was an ad in the paper. Puppy, free to good home. So here he is, darling! Merry Christmas!"

I looked at the puppy, who had already peed on the floor. He was part golden retriever and part something else, and he was truly enormous. "What is he? A St. Bernard or something?"

Arnold kneeled down and wrapped the puppy in

his arms. Then he kissed him. "I don't know *what* he is, but I love him. Don't you love him, Rita?"

"Yes, yes," I said, trying to recover myself. "What's his name?"

"I thought we might call him William Butler. After Yeats."

"Arnold," I said, "dearest. He's going to eat an awful lot. And he'll need shots at the vet."

"We'll manage," said Arnold happily. "We'll manage."

As I took the sweet rolls out of the oven, and poured us both some juice, I thought back over "Arnold's Menagerie," as I used to call it. When I first knew him, he had had a goat named Daisy, and then he had acquired three kittens. Now there was William Butler.

"I've never housebroken a puppy," I said, as William Butler peed on the floor again.

"We'll get a book on the subject," said Arnold, taking off his coat and muffler. "Do we have some hamburger or something? I forgot to get any dog food."

I went over to the fridge and took a hamburger out of the freezer compartment, trying to resign myself to the presence of William Butler, who was now chewing on Arnold's bedroom slipper. "Arnold," I said, "what time are you serving dinner?"

112

"Four o'clock. That's when I invited the Captain."

I stopped cold in my tracks. "What?"

"The Captain. I invited him for Christmas dinner."

I felt my heart sink—and then I felt a wave of anger. "Well, Arnold, for some reason you forgot to tell me that."

Arnold looked astonished. "Isn't it all right?"

"No!" I said. "It is not all right. I mean, my God, it's Christmas! Our first Christmas in our own home. Why does the Captain have to come?"

"Because he's alone in the world," said Arnold, "that's why. Really, Rita, this is not very nice of you."

"I don't care if it's nice or not! We've only got a small roasting chicken. And he'll eat every bite of it."

Arnold came over and put his hands on my shoulders. "Rita, this is Christmas—and what Christmas means is peace on earth and good will toward men."

"Does it also mean going hungry? Because you know he'll eat up all the food, and drink all the booze, and get tight. And then he'll spin his goddam yarns about Hong Kong!"

Arnold took William Butler in his arms and went to sit by the fire. "This is not worthy of you, Rita."

113

"I don't care, I just don't! Don't *I* have rights too? Aren't I a human being? I mean, God, Arnold, once—just once—something has to go my way. All I do is work, and sleep, and get up to go to work again, while *you* fool around on the beach. I can't support you forever! I'm sick of it!"

The minute the words were out of my mouth, I regretted them. Arnold's face had turned ashen. He put the puppy down on the floor. "I didn't know you felt that way."

"Forget it. Today's not the day to talk about it."

"On the contrary. I think we should talk about it. I didn't know you were unhappy."

"I'm not unhappy! I'm just . . . angry, that's all. Oh God, oh God, let's forget it."

But the words had been said, and all during the day they hung in the air between us. Arnold played with William Butler for a while, and then he started to prepare the meal—the same meal we had had at Thanksgiving, only with homemade tarts for dessert instead of apple pie. At four o'clock, R.W. Moss arrived, walking unsteadily, and bearing a bottle of Irish whiskey. "Noel, Noel!" cried Captain Moss. "Peace on earth to us all!"

So there we were—me and Arnold, and an oversized puppy, and a drunken sea captain—having our Christmas dinner. The radio blared its carols, and the snow fell, and R.W. Moss ate most of the

114

food. "Another helping?" Arnold would ask politely. "Don't mind if I do," the Captain would reply, heaping food on his plate.

My God, I thought, has my life really come down to this? Being jealous of how much another person *eats*? What has happened to me? Why have I turned into a shrew? Things could be so beautiful, except that they're not. And, dammit, the reason is me. But I don't know what to do about it.

"A toast!" cried Captain Moss, raising his glass of whiskey. "A toast to my dear shipmates Arnold and Rita! May the wind always be kind to you, may you find shelter from the storm, and may the good Lord shine down upon you like the sun!"

THE NEXT MORNING, Arnold walked into town and bought a collar and leash for William Butler, and also some dog food. Fortunately, he got a ride with a neighbor on the way back. Then he took William Butler down to the beach for a walk. It was a freezing day, with a dull gray sky, and by afternoon sleet was pelting our windows. Through the gloom I could see the ferry going back and forth. The ever-present sea gulls wheeled and cried.

Arnold was restless and distracted. He played

with the puppy, but I could see that his heart wasn't in it. He read a book and put it down. He went back to the beach for a walk. R.W., he said, was dozing in his little booth by the ferry slip, done in by our festivities.

By afternoon Arnold was so agitated that I asked him to sit down and talk to me. "What is it?" I asked him. "What's wrong?"

He looked at me, a long steady look—as if he was probing my soul. "Rita," he said, "I think you should go home for a while. To your parents."

"What?"

"You've been unhappy here. Why not take a few weeks at home and see how it suits you?"

"Jesus!" I said. "Whatever put that into your mind, Arnold? I mean, really!"

"I think we both need time to think."

"To think about what, for God's sake?"

"Us. About whether or not we have a future."

Well, that one stopped me cold. Dead cold. Because I knew that he meant it. I could have killed myself for what I had said to him yesterday. What a mistake.

"Arnold . . ."

"We need some time away from each other. We've both lost perspective somehow."

"But what about you? Who will take care of you?"

"You're not my mother, Rita."

No, I thought, and I'm not your child, either. But who I *am* in this relationship, I'll be darned if I know.

"I don't want to leave here. It's my home."

"Go back to your parents for a while. Try it out."

"But that's such an admission of defeat!"

"Only if you make it so."

"I won't go, Arnold."

"Yes, you will," he said. "For me."

So the next day I packed some clothes, and the manuscript of *All the Slow Dances*, and then I called my mother and said that I was coming home for a little vacation. "It's just for a few weeks," I said coolly. "Arnold needs privacy because he's working so hard on his book."

But it *was* an admission of defeat, and I felt awful about it. Because I didn't know how I would face my parents after all we'd been through.

My mother came and got me that afternoon. And as I walked out of the house with my suitcase, there were tears in her eyes. Arnold stood on the front porch with William Butler in his arms. "Two weeks," I said to him. "That's all. Two weeks, and then I come back. God, Arnold, how are you going to housebreak William Butler?"

"He'll be housebroken by the time you return," Arnold replied. "If you return."

We didn't kiss or anything. We just looked at each other for a long moment. Then I was in my mother's car, driving to town. And I'll say this much for Mom, she didn't ask any questions. All she said was "It's so wonderful to see you again. I'm so happy."

I thought that my father would be at the auto shop, but when we pulled into the driveway, I saw that his car was there. And suddenly I felt very nervous. Mortimer, the dog, was in the front yard and barked happily when he saw me. My dad came to the front door.

"There's my baby," he said. "There's my girl."

He embraced me—a kind of bear hug—and I was so glad to see him that I wanted to cry. "I'm just home for a few weeks," I explained. "A little vacation."

"Good girl," my father muttered. "A good brave girl."

I could tell that he thought Arnold and I had broken up, but I didn't have the strength to explain that we hadn't. And soon we were all in the kitchen, laughing and talking, and catching up on the news. It was just like the old days, just like I had never been away.

My aunt Peggy, said my mother, had gotten a promotion at her job. My grandmother was thinking of coming up from Florida in the spring. "And

I made slipcovers for the living room furniture," said Mom. "Come and have a look."

As though they were giving me a guided tour, my parents led me around the house. New slip-covers on the furniture, a new, inlaid coffee table. And, my God, how luxurious it all seemed. Carpets on the floor, and central heating, and television, and the smells of a pot roast coming from the kitchen. "There are new curtains in your room," Mom said to me. "I hope you like them."

She opened the door to my room, and I just stood there, staring. A pink-and-white room with stuffed animals on the bed, and posters on the walls. My high school graduation picture, framed. My old rolltop desk with its scuffed-up chair. My seashell collection. On the windowsill sat my Raggedy Ann doll.

It was a child's room, but where the child had gone I wasn't sure. "Doesn't it look nice?" my mother said to me. "We've kept it just as it was."

My mom served us a beautiful meal that night, and then we all sat in the living room and watched television. A game show, a situation comedy. An interview with a Playboy bunny who had had a breakdown after her Playboy Club went bust. My dad lit one of his expensive cigars. My mom worked on a sweater she was knitting for him. No one mentioned Arnold.

"Guy came into the shop the other day," my father was saying, "and offered to sell me an old Morgan. Wooden frame, would you believe it? Rosewood dashboard. I'm thinking of buying it."

I was sitting next to him on the couch. "You'd look great in a Morgan," I said. "Very sporty."

"You know me," he replied, "a sucker for the oldies. Show me an Aston Martin, an old Sunbeam Talbot, and I'm a goner."

Mom held up the sweater she was knitting. "Do you like this?" she asked me. "I think it's kind of original."

The sweater had autumn colors woven through it—gold, red, green. "Yeah," I said, "it's really nice." She went back to her knitting. The television continued.

We're running out of things to say, I thought. Any minute now they'll break down and ask me about Arnold, about the Ferry House.

"I hear you're working for an authoress," my dad said.

I giggled. "She's not an *authoress*, Daddy. Just a children's book writer. She's very successful."

"So what do you do for her? Typing?"

"Among other things, yes."

"Well, it's a job. But I want to see you in college next year, sweetie. I really do."

"Let's talk about that another time," I said, getting to my feet. "I want to go to bed now."

My father rose to his feet and embraced me. "It's good to have you home," he said. "Really wonderful."

My mom came into my room with me, and as I started to undress, she said, "Why, Rita!"

"Yes?" I said. "What is it?"

"You've lost so much weight!"

"I have?"

"Why yes, darling, you have. Haven't you noticed it yourself?"

"No. I mean, yes, I have. I mean, my clothes *have* been loose on me lately."

"We must weigh you tomorrow. How did you lose so much?"

I thought for a moment. "The bike," I said slowly. "That goddam bike."

"What, darling?"

"Nothing," I said. But privately I was thinking that "sweet are the uses of adversity." It was a quote that Arnold was fond of.

As though I were five years old, my mother tucked me into bed and kissed me—and then she left the room. I lay there for a while, listening to the murmur of the TV in the living room and thinking, I'm home, I'm home.

121

But it wasn't true. Because all I could see in my mind was Arnold on the porch of the Ferry House holding William Butler in his arms. And all I could think of was the fact that Arnold would be sleeping alone tonight. Well, not exactly. He would probably take William Butler to bed with him. But *I* wouldn't be there, and that was the strangest part of all. What is home, I asked myself? People, or things, or a bit of both?

I looked across the room. My Raggedy Ann doll was shining in the moonlight, as she sat on the windowsill. She had a big smile on her face.

THIS IS JUST AN experiment, I said to myself, when I woke up the next morning. Just an experiment. In two weeks you'll go back to Arnold and the vacation will have done you good. I mean, my God, Arnold's only three miles away! You can go back whenever you want. You can phone him every day.

But I didn't phone him. Instead, I went shopping with my mother, to buy some new jeans and a sweater, and then I went to work at the Quad's. The Quad had obviously had a busy holiday, because she was so hung over she could hardly speak.

"I have a virus," she said stiffly. "I'm lying down in my room."

Right, I thought, and the name of the virus is scotch. However. It was sort of nice to have her out of the way. Humming to myself, I cleaned the living room and put masses of dirty dishes into the dishwasher. I mopped the kitchen floor. I took out the garbage.

At least twenty times that day, I thought of phoning Arnold. I kept seeing him there alone, rattling around the house, playing with the puppy, walking down to the ferry to talk to the Captain. I saw him having a solitary dinner and reading a book in the chair by the fire. I saw William Butler peeing all over the floor.

It was so strange to be back home, so strange. And my feelings about it were conflicted. Part of it seemed wonderful, but most of it didn't fit me anymore. I kept looking at that Raggedy Ann doll, with her perpetual smile, and thinking, the little girl who owned *you* is gone, kiddo. . . . My mom was waiting on me hand and foot, and that made me uncomfortable too. For the very first time in my life, I realized how spoiled I had been as a child. For the very first time, I saw how much they had invested in me. I don't mean money. I mean hopes, dreams, vicarious feelings, fantasies. My parents had lived their whole lives through me, and for what? I would never be what they wanted —a pretty college freshman, soon to marry a handsome college boy—because I could only be myself. And yet, it was so touching. All my mom could talk about was clothes, and how much weight I had lost, and how many things she wanted to buy me. All my dad could talk about was college.

The three of us would sit in the living room after dinner, and the familiarity of it all was both wonderful and sad. My mother kept knitting that sweater. My father smoked his cigars.

And still, they did not mention Arnold.

I went to the auto shop and looked at the Morgan my dad wanted to buy. Mom took me to the hairdresser to have my hair cut. One night, they took me out to dinner at The Cooper Hotel. Another night, the three of us went to the movies. I worked for the Quad, and I slept in my old bed at night, and whenever the phone rang I was sure it was Arnold. But it never was. Arnold was holding still.

Another thing. My classmates from Peterson High were home for Christmas vacation, and a few of them phoned me. Even tiny Christopher Flynn phoned, and asked me out for a date. A date! The words sounded antiquated. "How's Middlebury?" I asked Christopher over the phone. "Neat," he said solemnly. "Very very neat."

My friend Corry Brown was home too, from Vassar, and so we agreed to meet in the city one Saturday for lunch. Wearing my blue jeans and an old coat, I went into town on the bus for this occasion. Corry had once lived in Sag Harbor, but now her parents lived on Manhattan's West Side, in a new and trendy neighborhood near the Museum of Natural History. Corry and I had decided to meet at a place called Jason's, and even though she was sitting at a table near the door when I walked in, I didn't recognize her. Corry, my old friend from grammar school, had changed.

I mean, there she was, dressed in faded Levi's, and wonderful boots, and a heavy wool poncho. There she was—her curly hair cut short, wearing dark glasses and smoking a long black cigaret. The words "radical chic" came to my mind at once, though I don't know from where. Corry had definitely changed.

To begin with, her vocabulary was different. Everything was "unreal" or "outrageous." Everything was "a hoot." She talked on and on about her professors at Vassar. She talked about "Psych One," which was taught by an outrageous person named Mr. Fellows. "He's just too outrageous," Corry said to me. "He has blue hair."

"Blue?"

I was sipping a Coke and Corry was sipping herb tea. We had both ordered sandwiches, but they hadn't arrived yet.

"Well, not exactly blue," she said. "But he does have gray hair, and most of us think that he tints it! He's so outrageous. I wish you could meet him."

I tried to picture myself on the Vassar campus, being introduced to a professor with blue hair, and couldn't. "I . . . I guess you really like college," I said to her. "I guess it's interesting."

"Well, yes," she said, blowing a stream of smoke into the air. "It *is* interesting. The teachers are much better than I had thought. There's Mr. Fellows, and there's my English teacher, Miss Dorian. We call her Dorian Gray. It's a hoot."

Our sandwiches arrived, and I began to eat mine. I felt very depressed. "Are you still active in the women's movement?" I asked. "Still working with women's groups?"

Corry gazed at me through her dark glasses. "Well, yes, of course. But what I'm really involved with right now is a freshman studies group on international terrorism. It's a very important group. *Very.*"

I had an image of Corry and her group taking off for the Middle East. I had a picture of them fighting, commando style, in the hills of Tripoli.

"Interesting," I said.

"More than interesting," she replied. "We're trying to get at the roots of the whole thing, studying Arab culture and all that. The teacher is unreal." She took a bite of her sandwich. "Look, Rita, what about *you*? You haven't said a word about yourself."

I sighed and attempted—briefly—to bring Corry up to date about my life. About Arnold, and the Ferry House, and our poverty. About the Quad, and about the fact that I was living at home for a few weeks. "It's just an experiment. Arnold thought we both needed some breathing space."

Corry looked at me. "You know, I don't want to sound like your mother or anything, but I was disturbed when you turned Hofstra down. I thought it was a bad decision."

"You did?"

"Of course I did! You're a talented writer, Rita. College would have been good for you."

"A person doesn't have to go to college to be a writer."

"That's not what I mean. It's just that the whole *cachet* of college is so important. So vital."

"Cachet?" I said in amazement. "Look, Corry, why don't you take off those dark glasses? We're not in Florida."

127

She took off her sunglasses. "I think it was a mistake," she said flatly. "I think you should have gone to Hofstra. And what about Arnold? What is he up to these days?"

"Well . . . he's still working on his book. And he walks on the beach a lot."

"And that's all?"

"Of course it's not all!" I said angrily. "He plays the organ twice a month in a local church. A week before Christmas, he even gave a concert."

I could see that Corry wasn't digging any of this. She was too Vassar now. Too outrageous. "Look," I said, "I don't expect you to understand any of this. I mean, at the moment, you and I are in different worlds."

Which said it all. Because this was not the Corry from the old days, but a new Corry who used words like cachet and was studying terrorism in the Middle East. Sad, sad, sad. We just didn't connect anymore. And I felt as lonely as a person on a raft, drifting out to sea. I sat there with her for another half hour, but in my mind I was on that raft in the middle of the Atlantic. When we parted, I was as depressed as I had ever been in my life.

The minute I got home, two hours later, I went to the dictionary and looked up that effing word "cachet." It meant exactly what I thought.

19

TWO WEEKS HAD PASSED and I had not heard from Arnold. And, unfortunately, my parents were acting like I was home for good. Routine—that terrible trap—had taken over the three of us, and we ate together, and watched TV, and went shopping like automatons. Happy automatons, but there you have it. By day, I wrote "Hospital News" and worked for the Dragon Lady. By night, after dinner, I worked on *All the Slow Dances*. I had told my parents that I was writing a novel—and, impressed, they left me alone in the evenings. With the murmur of the TV going on in the other room, I wrote and wrote.

It was a good novel, the story of Arnold and me, and I liked every single thing about it. Told in the first person, it is the story of a small-town girl who falls in love with a man who can only be called *un original*. The man is older than the girl, and poverty-stricken, and the parents disapprove. There are scenes in Europe, after the man has taken flight. I had made him a painter instead of a writer, and I had changed a few other things too, but it was definitely autobiographical.

I had been working on this book for over a year and had only done ninety pages. Nevertheless. The writer, Arnold was always saying, is the person who writes, and sticks to it, and does not give up.

The only thing was . . . . I did not know how the book was going to end.

Two weeks, then three. And though I sent my paycheck from the Quad to Arnold every week, there was no reply from him—which gave me terrible anxieties. Did he miss me at all? Was he getting used to my absence? He had said that William Butler would be housebroken by the time I returned, *if* I returned. God.

I would lie in bed at night and think about Arnold, and my heart would hurt. Because an experiment is only an experiment. How long was this going to continue? And what was the point of the whole thing? Arnold had told me to take these weeks to think about our situation, and I was trying to do that—but the only thing that came to mind was that marriage, so-called, had turned me into a shrew. I *hated* myself that way. It ruined my entire self-image.

Then, one evening, my father came into my room. Without knocking.

"Are you busy, honey?" he asked. Which was a superfluous question, since I was sitting at my desk, typing away on my Royal portable.

"Uh, no," I said, distracted. "What is it?"

Cigar in mouth, my father looked around the room. Then he chose a chair and sat down on it.

He seemed uncomfortable. "I don't want to disturb you."

"Yes?" I said. Because I wanted to continue my work.

"Sweetheart," said my father, "your mother and I were talking a little while ago, talking about you, and I think we have to come to some kind of decision here. I mean, are you going to stay with us or not? You know we want you here, baby, and you know that we love you. But we have to know your plans."

"I . . . I don't have any plans yet," I said. "This is just a trial separation between Arnold and me. An experiment."

It was the first time since I had been home that I had used the word "Arnold." My father winced.

"I'm counting on your going to college next year."

"Sorry," I replied. "There's no chance of that."

My father took the cigar out of his mouth. It wasn't lit. It was just his security blanket, something to hold on to. "Rita . . ."

"Please, Daddy. Let's not have this conversation again. I'm writing a novel, and I live with Arnold Bromberg, and I'm not going away to college. Those are the facts, and I can't change them."

"Then why did you come home to us?"

"Because I needed some time to think about my life. And Arnold needed some time too. We still love each other, we just needed to separate for a while."

Tears came into my father's eyes. "You're throwing your life away, baby. Throwing it away like an old shoe."

"No, Daddy, I'm not. It's just that you and I see things differently. And it will never change."

My father pulled his chair close to mine. "Do you know how much I love you?" he said.

"Yes. I think so."

"Well then, if you know that, don't break my heart. And don't break your mother's heart, either. Your fella's a *loser*, Rita, an all-time loser. He'll be writing that book for the rest of his life. And he will never, ever, support you."

And then—as though a light had gone on in my head—I saw the whole thing. And the clarity of it was astounding. I saw that my father was right, but that I was right too. Yes, Arnold would probably never finish his book, and yes, I would have to support him for the rest of my life, and yes, Arnold Bromberg was a character and an oddball. *But what the hell was wrong with that?* What did it matter *who* brought money into the house, and what did it matter where we lived or what we owned? The point—the goddam point of the whole thing— was that Arnold and I were not just committed to each other, we were also committed to ourselves.

132

"To be married is to be the guardian of another person's solitude," I had read somewhere. "To be married is to allow another person to change and grow." What I wanted for Arnold Bromberg was exactly what he wanted for me—freedom to be oneself.

"Thank you, Daddy," I said.

"Huh?" he replied. "For what?"

By way of replying, I went over and kissed him. And late that night, when he and my mother were asleep, I wrote Arnold a letter. "I love you," the last part of the letter said, "but I also love myself. I want a great life for you, and for me as well. We are good for each other, Arnold, and I'm committed to you, and I'm ready to come home now. Rita."

TWO NIGHTS LATER, as my parents and I sat in the living room watching television, the doorbell rang. "For goodness' sake," said my mother. "Who would it be at this hour?"

She disappeared down the hall, opened the front door, and there was a long silence. When she came back to the living room, Arnold Bromberg was with her.

My father rose to his feet and stared at Arnold,

and I did the same. For a long while the four of us simply stood there. "I've come for Rita," said Arnold. "Good evening."

I had to stifle a laugh, because it was like he was saying, "I've come for my laundry," or something. Then, after the desire to laugh had disappeared, a lump came into my throat. "Hello, darling," I said.

"Hello, Rita," he replied.

And still the four of us stood there, like people in a film that has been stopped in the middle. Stood there, not knowing what to do. But at last my mother, pulling herself together, said, "Won't you sit down, Mr. Bromberg?"

"Thank you," said Arnold. "I will."

He looked so wonderful, dressed in dark trousers and a heavy maroon sweater, a muffler round his neck. His clear eyes gazed at the three of us. His hands were folded in his lap.

"Well . . ." my father began.

Arnold gazed at my father in a neutral kind of way. "I'm taking Rita home with me tonight," he said, "and I know how this will make you feel, Mr. Formica. But our house is only a few miles down the road, so I hope that you will come to visit. I'd like to have you in our lives, you know. I'd welcome your friendship."

My father opened his mouth to speak, thought better of it, and closed it again.

"So," said Arnold, "that about says it, I think. We'd like you both to come and visit very soon, and be a part of our lives and our happiness." He turned to me. "Rita," he said gently, "get your things."

"Right," I said, "right." And I hurried off to my room.

It took me a while to get my stuff together, and when I returned to the living room, my father was actually *talking* to Arnold. Talking haltingly, but talking all the same. What had occurred during my absence I could not imagine, but something had definitely changed.

"The wife tells me that that house of yours needs some work done on it," my father was saying. "She says that the roof is a little shot."

"It's true," said Arnold. "We had some work done on it in the beginning, but it still leaks a bit. When the rain comes from the east."

"What kind of shingles?" asked my father.

"Asbestos," Arnold replied.

"Well, maybe I could lend you a hand," said my father gruffly. "I'm a pretty good carpenter."

I don't *believe* this, I thought. It isn't happening.

"Thank you, sir," said Arnold. "And we do accept, don't we, Rita?" He had his arm around my shoulders.

"We do, we do," I said happily. "Come over on

the weekend," I said to my dad. "We'll go over the place together."

I kissed my father good-bye, and I kissed my mother good-bye. "Now remember," I said, "that you're coming to see us this weekend. Arnold will cook dinner for us. Something nice."

Arnold and I walked out to the street. But instead of leading me down the block, he led me over to a white car. "What's this?" I said.

"Our car," he replied.

"What?"

"I have bought us a car. Get in."

Sure enough, there was William Butler in the front seat, twice as big as when I had last seen him, and wagging his tail madly. "I don't believe this!" I said. "How did you buy a car?"

"That," said Arnold smiling, "is a subject for another day."

But Arnold, I wanted to say, I lost weight riding the goddam bike! You didn't have to buy a car! Truly, you didn't.

The car was a Dodge Colt, small and white, and in very good shape. All Arnold would say about it was that he had bought it in Riverhead. "Does it really run?" I asked.

By way of replying, Arnold turned on the ignition and pulled away from the curb. The car was wonderful. Its engine purred. The seats were bright blue. "I love this car!" I said, as William Butler covered me with kisses. "It's tremendous!"

When we entered the house, I got a bit of a shock. Because so many things were different. There were now two bureaus for our clothes, instead of one, and the windows were neatly covered with sheets of plastic, to keep the cold out. "I fixed the refrigerator," Arnold said casually. "It no longer makes that funny noise."

I walked around the room, liking it, appreciating every bit of its lovely shabbiness. "Is the dog housebroken?" I said to Arnold. "The rug looks so clean."

"Almost, almost. I got a book on the subject."

"I like the new bureau," I said.

And still we did not kiss or embrace each other. "How did you get that car?" I asked.

"We'll talk about it in a minute. Do you want some pie and coffee?"

"Yes," I said, taking off my coat. "That would be wonderful."

Arnold lit two candles and we sat down at the table as he served up a fresh blueberry pie. William Butler had conked out on the rug. "I've made some changes in my life the past few days," said Arnold. "Do you want to hear about them?"

137

I took his hand. "Yes, darling. Of course."

Arnold stared over my head, the way he does when something means a lot to him. "Well," he began, "the first thing is that I stopped smoking two days ago, and that it's working. I'm not even having withdrawal. And the second thing is that I have a job."

I put down my fork. "A job?"

"Mr. Beasley, the organist at the church, is retiring soon. They want me to be organist and choirmaster."

"But how wonderful!"

"Yes, it is. The salary is small, but steady. I am also about to study bookbinding. In my spare time."

I started to laugh. "Bookbinding? Where could you study bookbinding in the Hamptons? What *is* bookbinding, for God's sake?"

"Just what you think it is, except that I'll be binding rare books. I met an antiquarian book dealer in Riverhead—and he gave me the idea."

"How did you buy that car?" I asked.

"All right, I'll tell you. I sold my Gordon Craig magazines in Riverhead—to Mr. Steinberg, the antiquarian book dealer. It was he who gave me the idea of bookbinding because his partner in the shop does it."

"Oh, no," I said, "not the Gordon Craig magazines. Oh, Arnold!"

138

A word here, to explain that Arnold's most beloved possessions were four hand-printed magazines by Edward Gordon Craig, the stage designer. Craig had been the lover of Isadora Duncan, and a great innovator. His hand-printed, hand-colored magazines, from 1890, were worth several thousand dollars. Arnold had owned them since college.

"Oh, Arnold. I feel terrible."

"No reason to," he said calmly. "I enjoyed them for many years, and now they'll go on to someone else. I used the money for a down payment on the car. However, we'll still have to pay something each month."

"I don't know what to say to you. You make me feel awful."

"But why? Changes *needed* to be made in our lives. It's just that I'd never lived with anyone before. I didn't know what was required."

"You make me want to cry."

"Well don't, sweetheart. Because we have a lot to do together. Didn't your letter to me say that change is the name of the game? The courage to change and grow?"

I came around to his side of the table and took his face in my hands. "You're an amazing person, Arnold. And I love you very much."

"Let's get married," he said. "In the spring."

21

THAT WINTER EVERYTHING opened up for Arnold and me. I don't mean that we didn't have problems—because this story is not a fairy tale—but the changes were tremendous. To begin with, my parents started coming over, and the fact that we let them participate in our lives made all the difference. Why hadn't I thought of that before? It was so simple, so simple. My mother gave me lots of stuff for the Ferry House and made curtains for the windows. My dad worked on the plumbing and the roof. On Sundays, they came to Sunday dinner. Sometimes, Arnold and I went to them. It wasn't living happily ever after, but it was *something*. The beginning of a life and a future.

The night Arnold had brought me home from my parents' house, we had talked for hours—and together we had vowed that we would both get up at six every morning and work on our books. He would work at his desk, which was a card table by the front window. I would work at the kitchen counter on a stool. And, by God, we did just that. I mean, it took a certain amount of discipline to get up that early, but we did, and for some reason his typewriter didn't bother me, nor mine him.

Well, let me tell you. Reality is obviously not what I say it is, or even what I think it is. Because every time that I decided things were one way, that winter, they would turn out to be another. For example, this relationship that was developing between my father and Arnold. In February there was a warm spell, so together the two of them went up on the roof to put on some shingles. As you may have guessed by now, Arnold is not exactly a master carpenter—so that gave my dad a certain advantage over him. Not that he flaunted it or anything. But I would hear the two of them up there, shouting away to each other, and sometimes the whole thing would break me up. "Hey, Bromberg, shake a leg!" my father would shout. "Get me those shingles!" "Yes, sir, on the double!" Arnold would shout back. An hour later the two of them would be back in the kitchen, for a beer, and I would watch them together in amazement.

What was it? That my dad had capitulated, or that Arnold was beginning to win him over? The latter, I think, because Arnold is very good with people when he decides to be. He would ask my father a million questions, about plumbing and carpentry—and about the Dodge Colt—and my father would light a cigar, lean back in his chair, and expound. The car, he decided, was in good shape for a secondhand job, but needed the wheels balanced. It would be very easy, he announced, to add a shower stall onto the house, around near the porch. On and

141

on—with Arnold nodding and listening, and my father being a big shot. But it was OK. It was even wonderful, because I saw that we were all going to make it now.

The winter passed. William Butler became housebroken and learned to come when he was called—which was great, because we could now let him run on the beach. Arnold worked on his book, and rehearsed the choir three times a week, and practiced the organ—and every Friday he would go into Riverhead to study bookbinding. As for me, I had gotten to page one hundred and fifty of my novel and could see some light at the end of the tunnel. I continued to work for the Quad, and the better I got to know her, the more my animosity disappeared. The Dragon Lady was lonely and did not have any real friends. The Dragon Lady also drank too much, and had a phobia about cats, and was obsessed with her haircut. Every week she would ask Shawn the hairdresser to change it just a little. She spent a lot of time on the phone with gay men.

"I'm getting married," I told her, "in May. Will you come?"

She looked up from the copy of *Harper's Bazaar* that she was reading. "Why, of course I'll come. What would you like for a wedding present?"

The question embarrassed me. "We don't need anything," I murmured. "We're fine."

She took off her glasses and sighed. Oddly enough, she was not working on a book at the moment. She was just hanging around the house reading magazines and drinking coffee and answering her mail. "I'll think of something," she said. "And Rita? I'm happy for you."

I looked up from my dusting, and saw that she meant it. She was happy for me, and she really did want to give me a wedding present. Strange, strange, strange. Reality was definitely not what I thought it was. Reality was . . . on a different plane.

22

WHEN I TOLD MY MOTHER that I wanted to be married on the ferry, she almost fainted. I mean, she had grown accustomed to many things in the past few months, but this one almost did her in. "Oh, no," she said to me. "You're not serious."

Well, all right, so it was an odd choice. But who ever said I was normal? I wanted to be married on the Shelter Island ferry, as it went back and forth, because the ferry was special to both Arnold and me. "But no one gets married on a ferryboat!" said my mother. "It's crazy!"

I sympathized with her, I really did. Because, like all mothers, she had visions of a church wedding, with me in a long white dress, and bridesmaids and bouquets of flowers. Etc. But I did not want that. I, Rita Formica, fat person and writer, wanted to be married on the Shelter Island ferry. And Arnold agreed.

There were long discussions between Arnold and me on ferryboat weddings vs. church weddings. There were long discussions, among all of us, on the propriety of the whole thing.

"What is this asshole idea!" my father bellowed. "I won't stand for it."

"Daddy," I said calmly, "this is not your wedding. It's mine."

"But Rita," said my mother, "it will look so strange to everyone."

"So who's everyone?" I replied. "The only people who matter is us."

"I will not pay for this nutty idea!" said my father. "Not one penny!"

But he did. And by the middle of April he had rented the ferryboat for forty-five minutes on the 10th of May. Arnold's parents were coming from Kansas, and my grandmother was coming up from Florida. Corry Brown would be the one bridesmaid—and Captain Moss, sober we hoped, would be best man. The Reverend Thomas, from the Episcopal church, would marry us. To please my par-

144

ents, I had agreed on a reception afterward—at their house.

Sag Harbor, in May, is very beautiful. The sky becomes a robin's-egg blue, and great white fluffy clouds sail by, and there are always a few early sailboats on the water, bending into the wind. The swans are just about to hatch their young, and fruit trees have burst into blossom. Suddenly everyone's lawn looks very green. The winter clothes get put away.

Early in April my mother had begun to make me a wedding dress. Not a long dress, but a very pretty one in rose-colored cotton. Long sleeves. A sash. Arnold would wear his one good dark-blue suit. After the ceremony, there would be champagne on the ferry. God, I prayed, please don't let it rain on May 10th. Please let the sun shine and the clouds float by. Let the swans hatch their eggs and sail past the ferryboat with cygnets. Let everything be perfect.

And it was. Because on the morning of May 10th, Arnold and I woke and looked out the window at a dazzling blue sky. Clouds like white castles, building and changing in the air. Flocks of cormorants, and the scent of flowering trees. Arnold took William Butler down to the ferry, for a walk. When he returned, he said that the Captain was sober.

I have not yet mentioned Arnold's parents here, but they were exactly what I had expected. Two sweet, gentle people from Topeka, Kansas. The Reverend Bromberg, who was retired, had snow-white hair and a beautiful smile. His wife was a kindly, nervous type who said "My word!" a lot. My word, she would say, what a cunning little house you live in. My word, how lovely Long Island is! But the point is, I liked them and they liked me. And they said *not a word* about my being younger than Arnold. All the Reverend Bromberg said to me was "It's about time that boy got married."

They stayed at The Cooper Hotel, while my aunt and grandmother stayed with my parents. And—oh yes—the Quad gave me a check for five hundred dollars. Would you believe it! Five hundred. It would pay for building the shower.

About a week before the wedding, I was over at my parents' house packing my stuff—the last things, the books and so forth—when I realized that my father was talking to a friend on the phone in the hallway. About Arnold. Here's how my father's side of the conversation went.

Bromberg's the name. Right, right. He's a writer. Pretty good, too, my daughter tells me. A very educated guy. Right. We're very happy about it. . . . (*laughter*) Right, right. They're getting married on the ferry. Listen, what can I tell you? Crazy kids, right? Yeah, Arnold Bromberg. He's a writer.

And then it was the afternoon of May 10th, and fifteen of us were gathered on the deck of the Shelter Island ferry. A perfect, sunny, shining day. My mother looking beautiful in a blue linen suit and a straw hat. My aunt, my grandmother, Miss Quadrangle, the Captain. God! It was all so lovely.

The Captain pulled up the gangplank, and the ferrymaster blew his horn, and we were off—on one of the shortest journeys in the world. Standing in a circle, everyone was suddenly very quiet. My father, dressed in his best suit, looked like he might weep.

"Dearly beloved," said Reverend Thomas. "We are gathered together . . ."

I tried to hear every word, and appreciate it, but I couldn't. Because all I could see was Arnold Bromberg, smiling at me, looking beautiful and distinguished in his one good blue suit. His eyes were the green of oceans and seas, and his cheeks, as always, were ruddy. As the minister's words continued, we just smiled at each other. "You look beautiful," he whispered.

"Do you, Rita, take this man to be . . ." A sail-

147

boat with a red sail approached us, and the two people on board waved. The wind rose, and the sails billowed, and the sailboat passed.

"And do you, Arnold, take this woman . . ." I listened to the words, but they kept slipping away from me, scooped up by the wind and taken out to sea. But it didn't matter because I knew them by heart anyway.

"I hereby pronounce you . . ." said Reverend Thomas. But Arnold and I were already in each other's arms, kissing, and it was as though we had never kissed before. And my father was crying, and my mother had just embraced Mrs. Bromberg. It was too much, too much.

There was only one bridesmaid, Corry, but I threw my bouquet to her all the same, and then there was laughter and champagne, and everyone hugging me. And how could I ever have believed that I wouldn't be happy on this earth, I ask you? How could I have been so crazy?

Arnold's father kissed him, and then slapped him on the back. My father and Arnold shook hands. "A toast, a toast!" people were saying, and I heard every word of those toasts and saw every single thing that was going on—but still there was a part of me that was elsewhere, far out on the water where all the important things of this earth were gathered. Sea and sky, and birds and wind, and the endless climbing clouds.

I sipped champagne from Arnold's glass. The ferry turned and headed back to our shore. It would keep shuttling between the two shores until the party was over. But Arnold and I, from our house, could watch it for years.

What I wanted to say to everyone, but couldn't, was that Arnold Bromberg had been right. The whole dance was one dance, and we were all a part of the universe, and there was *nothing*, ever, to be afraid of.

Yes, folks. Arnold Bromberg was right.

Lose yourself in award-winning teen fiction from

Laurel-Leaf

books!

__CAL CAMERON BY DAY,
SPIDER-MAN BY NIGHT
by A. E. Cannon 20313-9 $2.95

__CHARTBREAKER
by Gillian Cross 20312-0 $2.95

__GROW UP, CUPID
by June Oldham 20256-6 $2.95

__GUYS LIKE US
by Stuart Buchan 20244-2 $2.95

__THE ISLAND KEEPER
by Harry Mazer 94774-X $2.95

__THE WORLD IS MY EGGSHELL
by Philippa Greene Mulford ..20243-4 $2.95

At your local bookstore or use this handy page for ordering:

DELL READERS SERVICE, DEPT. DFC
P.O. Box 5057, Des Plaines, IL. 60017-5057

Please send me the above title(s). I am enclosing $_____.
(Please add $2.00 per order to cover shipping and handling.) Send
check or money order—no cash or C.O.D.s please.

Ms./Mrs./Mr. _____

Address _____

City/State _____ Zip _____

DFC-2/90

Prices and availability subject to change without notice. Please allow four to six
weeks for delivery.